GW00393652

Contents

Foreword 5

Journey's start 8

Hospital routine 10

Green shoots 11

Ups and downs 12

Hopeful but hampered 13

Conditional homecoming.....................................14

Results day 15

Sibling match!..17

Options and contradictions...................................18

Transplant – the final frontier...............................18

Royal visit!..20

Fame and reality...21

Fighting infection 22

A royal surprise...22

Media spotlight and normality 24

Fame and chemo 24

Hospital and drugs...26

A day to remember...27

Results day!...28

Blood counts down but not out 29

Doldrums and discussion......................................30

Homeward bound 32

Remission – how sweet the sound!.............................33

Scent of Christmas 35

Setback..36

Thankful this Christmas......................................37

New year, new plan 38

The day after tomorrow.......................................39

One Direction – no turning back 40

Conditioning and make up.....................................42

Day Zero 42

Days of Zero 43

Whose perspective?...44

A flicker.. 45

Half empty...46

And here is the better news..................................47

But here is the best news!...................................48

Poignant celebration...49

Groundhog Day 50

That was the week that was...................................51

Discharged! 52

Convalescing 53

Journeys' end?...54

A new chapter 55

This time it's serious 57

Exciting developments 58

War of attrition...59

Recovering..60

Onwards and upwards...............................68

Prayer and preparation 70

Fire with fire 71

Maintaining remission 72

Preparing for admission...........................73

T day..74

Post transplant and unexpected post 75

Summer days 76

Grow cells grow! 77

When negative is positive.........................78

Bad temperature stops play 79

Setbacks...80

Home; but not alone 81

Steady growth 82

Preparing for T Day...................................83

T Cells R Us...84

'One shall rout a thousand' 85

"Cautiously optimistic" 86

2013 and all that 88

T cells 30 : Leukaemia luv 88

New hope please 90

A question of ethics 91

Times and seasons 93

Something positive 94

Staying positive 95

Thumbs up 96

Last stop 98

Tanks and thanks 99

Down but not out 100

Change of course 102

This sucks! 104

Infections, decisions and our big G........................105

The longest night..107

Pain and awe...109

Remembrance Day – our fighter goes home 111

Raining in my heart 114

Eleven Eleven..117

Acknowledgements 120

About the authors 121

Foreword

'Faith for Fabian'. 'That's it!' I exclaimed. I had been searching for a title for my blog and I knew it had to sum up in a few words what the blog was about. This captured it perfectly – our faith as Christians and our son Fabian. I could never have imagined how that title would come to epitomise our family's journey as he fought to overcome leukaemia.

My blog actually began several years after Fabian's first diagnosis with Acute Lymphoblastic Leukaemia (ALL) back in July 2006. There wasn't much need for faith back then. We had been told the prognosis for a total cure was very high, around 85-90%. He was the 'right' age and was eligible for the UK ALL trial that was producing excellent outcomes. The treatment of chemotherapy was to last three years but most of this time would be spent at home on maintenance therapy whilst in remission. As for the 10% or so for whom chemo fails, that would be someone else. It's never your own child, is it?

This utopian view went reasonably to plan. Fabian achieved 'technical remission' a month into the treatment although a more detailed test known as MRD had indicated there was some residual disease in his bone marrow, implying that there was a greater risk of relapse than the 90% cohort. Again, we only ever thought it would be someone else's child and not our own that would be one of those very few. Indeed, he completed treatment in September 2009 and spent the best part of the next two years in full remission and enjoying normal life. No faith needed then. All that changed overnight when in August 2011, symptoms returned and a subsequent bone marrow test confirmed the worst – relapse.

That was when my idea of a blog was borne. And this is where it begins.

Darrell Bate
December 2020

SUNDAY, AUGUST 14, 2011

Journey's start

Welcome to my first entry of Faith4Fabian. It's actually
been more than 5 years since Fabian, our youngest son,
was first diagnosed with acute lymphoblastic leukaemia
(ALL) on July 6th 2006. I guess one can get apathetic
when things are going well. He appeared to be doing
very well since coming off treatment in September
2009. Then a couple of months ago he ran a couple of
high temperatures which turned out to be some viral
infections. Nothing too out of the ordinary although as
with any medical condition, these were reported to his
consultant at the Royal Marsden Hospital. She decided
to probe further with more in depth blood tests and
these indicated a strong likelihood of leukaemic blast
cells which she euphemistically described as ' we think
there is a problem and he needs to come into hospital as
you can'. So on Sunday 24th July he was duly admitted
and has remained there since that day.

Within a couple of days Fabian underwent surgery to
have a bone marrow aspirate (a sample of bone marrow
is taken from the hip) and a Hickman line implanted.
This is essentially 3 catheter tubes which are fed directly
into the heart though which all medication and medical
support is given. It's an amazing device which negates
the need for painful catheters although he will be
limited in what physical activities he can do whilst this
line is in place.

The aspirate confirmed the presence of blast cells (98%)
in the bone marrow but thankfully a secondary test to
see whether these were present in the spinal fluid - and
therefore the brain - proved negative. Due to the late
timing of his relapse he is deemed to be intermediate
rather than high risk. This means his treatment
protocol is only chemotherapy rather than radiotherapy
or stem cell transplant. The first phase of intensive
chemo began almost immediately on the 27th July and
will continue for 28 days. During this time he is

hospital-bound and loses all his natural immunity. For the budding oncologists among you, the drugs used are; vinchristine, mitoxanthene, methotrexate, dexamethasone, asparaginase and cotrixomale. These all carry side effects which vary between patients. Fabian initially had a lot of nausea and vomiting but the dexamethasone, a steroid, increases appetite so the desire to eat and feel sick complement each other! The main risk during this phase is infection. Most complications arise due to this cause rather than the cancer itself. The first sign is usually a spike in temperature. We have been told to expect many of these throughout his treatment but we are believing for better. That said, Fabian has already encountered an unexpected complication which is that he was found to have contracted cryptosporidiosis, a water-borne parasite that attacks the gut. This has been causing him extensive and prolonged diarrhoea and resulted in quite a bit of weight loss in the past two weeks. There is no effective cure, it's something that the body eventually attacks though of course in immune-deficient children this is much harder to achieve. For a time, the doctors needed to supply Fabian with nutrition via his line and he has been on a saline drip since admission. We parents have to care for his toileting needs and this has been quite wearing especially after multiple incidences during the night. However, in the past 24 hours he appears to be turning a corner so we are hopeful the worst is over. He is, however, required to remain in isolation until the risk of infection has passed. This does mean he gets a large room with ensuite all to himself but sadly does not get to see the other children or join them in the play room. It's been great, though, to have had a number of visitors including some of his friends and the difference in his demeanour is noticeable after only a short period when they visit. We are also exploring Skype as the most efficient form of communication since the mobile signals are dreadful on the ward. Possibly something to do with the lead-lined

walls?
Thanks for reading this and join us again next time!

MONDAY, AUGUST 15, 2011

Hospital routine

Finally, the diarrhoea is subsiding. Fabian even went through the night without an 'incidence' last night. Still, being on fluids constantly requires multiple uses of the 'peepot', each of which has to be carefully deposited in the sluice room for measuring and recording - a nurse's job can be a thankless one!

There are signs of his impending hair loss. Fabian is rather ambivalent about it, having experienced this all before but he's said he doesn't want to look like a baseball. But I guess will have to wear a baseball cap.

He's enjoyed having a few of his school friends visit in the last couple of days. Tired or not, he perks up and gets stuck into some serious play, turning his bed into legoland or a toy car park. The catheter lines inevitably get snagged and it's a bit like a game of Twister to get them untangled.

Tonight, staff and parents of Fabian's school gathered to pray for him and our family. Church members too, are providing ongoing prayer. It's humbling to have such spiritual support. Keep tarrying!

10pm - lights out.

SATURDAY, AUGUST 20, 2011

Green shoots

It's now Day 28 at the Marsden and a fairly uneventful few days since our last entry. The effects of the crypto bug continue to subside and Fabian's stools are now described by their firmness rather than their looseness. We anticipate he will not be considered infectious for too much longer, although perversely that may mean he has to give up his luxury isolation penthouse! The noticeable effect of this bug has been significant weight loss - around 5.5kg since his admission or 18% of his original body mass. It's tough when you see your own child start to resemble those images from the famine in Somalia. The doctors, of course, do not let such emotions undermine their professionalism and they are happy with his progress, having as they do, an armoury of clinical support weapons to keep him healthy. Having just completed one round of antibiotics, Fabian spiked another temperature so the whole cycle resumed again. Not that he is particularly aware of the cocktail of drugs being pumped into him with clockwork regularity. We joke about his 3 intravenous catheters representing premium, premium plus and diesel. Never put the wrong drug down the wrong line! He is sometimes given a choice of oral (tablet or liquid) or intravenous ingestion. That can be quite a hard decision for a 9-year-old and he questions the colour, taste, size and frequency of the drug. The nurses are very patient and would make excellent saleswomen, extolling the virtues of each type. On one occasion he opted for potassium by tablet as it resembled a large smartie. It would have been better swallowed not chewed as the taste was so odious it caused him to bring up a bedpan full.

Each day is punctuated by a series of routine tasks; BP, weight and temperature obs every 3 hours, blood test, doctors rounds and examination, multiple medications, saline renewal and 3 meals. Who said the life of an

11

oncology patient was boring? Visitors always break the monotony and these are eagerly awaited by Fabian who gives them a telling off if they are 'late'.

The bulk of the intensive chemo is over for this first phase of treatment. His WBC count is starting to rise and this is the 'green shoots' of recovery that mean they can think about letting him home. I asked him what surprise he would like that on that day but after he told me he was annoyed because he realised it would no longer be a surprise!

Fabian would like to thank all the readers of this blog and do remember to send him a message via Guestbook!

FRIDAY, AUGUST 26, 2011

Ups and downs

Day 34. Still at the Hotel Marsden where it's starting to feel like an episode of The Suite Life of Zack and Cody (for those Disney Channel fans among you). Except that today Fabian left his room for the first time in 20 days, alas only to visit the 1st floor for an ultrasound and CT scan. Still, it was a taste of freedom for him and he is increasingly demanding to go home. This could be potentially imminent but a persistent temperature keeps recurring, thus postponing the possibility. We're very pleased to say his appetite has returned though he can be very choosy about his taste. At the moment he has a craving for Macdonald's. This necessitates frequent drives to the nearest branch in Sutton, then smuggled in past the nurses!

His cryptosporidiosis is now being treated with nitaoxanide and I think we have seen the worse effects subside, not to return. It has been a trial to see this attack overcome. We don't know which future ones he may face, but on good advice we are not thinking too far ahead, just trying to make the days count. Next week Fabian undergoes a further general anaesthetic for an intrathecal injection. At this point they will draw a bone marrow sample for the critical MRD test. This provides doctors with the most accurate prognostic feature to determine his response to the chemotherapy and whether, ultimately a bone marrow transplant is needed. Please join us in believing and praying that this will not be the case.

WEDNESDAY, AUGUST 31, 2011

Hopeful but hampered

Today was due to be the much-anticipated Day 35 MRD test. But it was not to be. Fabian's blood count was simply too low for the test to produce a meaningful result. Basically, the bone marrow needs to be back in full swing when they take the sample rather than in a dilapidated state. A new date for the procedure has been set for next Tuesday but we have also been told he should be well enough to go home for the weekend. I can imagine how prisoners must feel when they face a parole board. In Fabian's case it's doctors who'll decide and he knows if he's not on his best health he'll be back inside!

Another event to report is the decision to go ahead with inserting a nasal gastric tube. This will happen tomorrow without anaesthetic instead of the original plan to do when he is next under general. The previous time they did this was particularly unpleasant and he is really brave to agree to this again. The urgency for this procedure is that his weight loss is such that he needs to supplement his food intake with overnight 'feeds' which will be a milkshake cocktail of nutrients and calories. Cool or what?

We've been advised that the evil Dr Crypto bug is still virulent and may well persist in his body for some years to come, such is it's resistance to all known antibiotics. It could also mean he remains in isolation during most of his hospital stays. This sobering news has eclipsed the fact that he has otherwise been coping incredibly well, keeping up his appetite despite perpetual diarrhoea and nausea.

Tonight, we met a young doctor who told us that years before she had been a marrow donor for her own brother and this had led her into medicine. Coincidentally, Oli, now 17, took and passed her UKCAT medical test today which takes her a huge step closer to fulfilling her own aspiration to become a doctor. On hearing the news, Fabian was keen to ask if she would be his doctor! Join us next time as we journey together in faith for Fabian.

MONDAY, SEPTEMBER 5, 2011

Conditional homecoming

True to their promise, Fabian was indeed let out last Friday afternoon. He arrived home to a heroes welcome, well it was just the 6 of us but it felt great to have him back. He was immediately observant, noting that our chick was now a full-grown cockerel and the grass needed mowing. Alas, he is only being let out during day times as his blood count hasn't recovered sufficiently. He needs to reach the 0.2 neutrophils baseline which to date has eluded him. This too means the MRD test is further postponed so we live from blood test to result to blood test.

Fabian's NG tube is a rather obvious feature (why can't it be flesh coloured?) but is proving the best way to pump in the calories and his weight is steadily climbing. The diarrhoea has finally abated (amen) and he has had no more temperature spikes. Progress indeed!

Oli, Ben and Cassia start school again this week so some sense of normality will return. It has felt like the most protracted summer holidays within memory. Full board at the Hotel Marsden will remain our enduring recollection of 2011.

On a different note, as the world reflects on the forthcoming 10th anniversary 9/11, please also remember that September is Childhood Cancer Awareness month with September 12th being named Childhood Cancer Awareness day. Go to www.curesearch.org to read more.

Thanks, as ever for reading and see you next time.

THURSDAY, SEPTEMBER 8, 2011

Results day

Quite a lot has happened; one minute the pace of change can seem glacial, the next, it's warp speed. Read on..

Firstly, the decision not to proceed with the MRD and bone marrow aspirate was reversed and this went ahead on Tuesday, including intrathecal chemo to the CNS (central nervous system). By then, Fabian's count had reached the 0.2 'freedom' threshold so he was allowed to go home *for the night*! So armed with a small pharmacy of medicine and equipment, Lydia arrived home and set about creating ward conditions around the house. Hand washing and toilet flushing has never been so enforced. Fabian requires a nightly feed via his NG tube although we set the pump up incorrectly which resulted in the darned thing bleeping on the hour every hour. Much like a real ward, actually..

Our consultant had asked us to come in Wednesday morning as she expected to have the results of the BM (though not the MRD). I can say it's a very different feeling to that of awaiting your child's exam results not least as the outcome would be potentially far more significant. As it turned out, their findings were inconclusive. On the plus side they found no blast cells but were equally unable to detect sufficient healthy stem cells to determine if he was in remission. other features such as platelets, WBC, cell morphology and Fabian's clinical state all point towards a positive chemo response - but we will have to wait until they repeat the whole process again next week to be sure. We also received unconfirmed results from the Anthony Nolan Trust concerning the sibling donor blood test which I will share in a later post.

Secondly, we had expected to be readmitted onto the ward to start the next block of chemo but, again, in a surprise move, the doctors decided to discharge us and to resume chemo in a week's time once his counts have improved. So we have had to vacate 'Room 101' and ship out a whole summer's worth of accumulated accoutrements. Hazel, the ward cook, will no doubt miss the daily meal orders from Fabian, which, after having exhausted every combination of the a la carte menu, he had resorted to saying, 'don't you know by now?'.

A particular blessing for us to have the whole family together this weekend is that it coincides with both our birthdays and we have much to celebrate. Do get in touch if you are free Saturday afternoon/evening to come along to an impromptu party!

PS Fabian's very excited to have had over 100 visits to this blog. Do remember to sign the guestbook!

THURSDAY, SEPTEMBER 15, 2011

Sibling match!

Welcome back to our journal after a week of living a normal life having Fabian at home. He's been really flourishing in his own environment and generally bossing us all around and of course, none of us mind. We were blessed to have a good number of friends come to an impromptu birthday/homecoming party on Saturday. Those who had last seen Fabian at his lowest point were stunned by his improvement. So now he is back 'inside' ready to start the next block of chemo - the deadly methotrexate. The pattern is likely to be 4 days in hospital/3 days at home for the next month subject to - well anything. On Wednesday he underwent the follow up bone marrow aspirate, now that his counts had recovered sufficiently. This will, in a few days provide the first confirmation of whether he is in remission. We believe that he deserves to be - no-one deserves cancer, least of all a child. But years of fighting this disease have made us more pragmatic about the eventual outcome. The possibility of a BMT is the elephant in the room. But that thought has just become a whole lot easier to digest upon the news we received that BOTH our girls are confirmed 100% matches! Thank you Jesus! What a privilege it may be for one of them, though let us all continue to believe that a transplant will not be required. Interestingly, the news came just as Oli was about to submit her UCAS application to study medicine - perhaps a sign she is following the right path?

TUESDAY, SEPTEMBER 20, 2011

Options and contradictions

A quick update to let you know there has been no confirmed result from last weeks' bone marrow but we are told they managed to draw off a sufficient sample to send to the labs. This is wonderful news as it keeps our options open but it's fair to say the doctors are 'more positive' about the transplant route now they know they have a guaranteed sibling match. The forums on ALL Relapse are very helpful on this subject but somewhat contradictory. It seems that for everyone who has had a positive outcome with chemo, another says they wish they had gone to transplant. And at the centre of this is our 9 year old son who has to trust every decision that is made regarding his health.

It's likely Fabian will be home tomorrow for a few days before starting a course of cyclophosphamide. This drug is known to affect fertility so we will again trust and pray against these side effects. He's in good spirits and piling the weight back on. Cassia's been good company to him, having been marooned at the hospital for the past couple of days as pick-ups have been awkward.

I'm signing off now but don't you forget to sign the guestbook!

TUESDAY, SEPTEMBER 27, 2011

Transplant – the final frontier

When I began this journal I recognised that there would times of writing painful entries alongside those that were more upbeat. This is such a time. As mentioned last time, we had been expecting results of the latest bone marrow aspirate. For a number of days it has felt like the sword of Damocles hanging over us and I had a

resignation in my spirit that the news, when it came
would not be good. Prior to this Lydia and I had shared
in church and received prayer. Ironically, the pressures
of being in a Christian community make you not want to
let people down or see their faith rocked when news is
disappointing. In reality, few things outside our control
go the way we expect and wishful thinking can
sometimes be mistaken for faith. So to come to the
point, our consultant confirmed today that sadly Fabian
was not in remission, having 10% blast cells and a
positive MRD signalling that his disease is drug
resistant. The chemotherapy therefore has failed and he
will now require a bone marrow transplant. This is the
news we never imagined having to hear about our own
son. Someone else's - but not ours. The odds are
impossibly low; each year approximately one in 25,000
UK children under 14 contract leukaemia, one in a
hundred thousand relapse and one in two hundred
thousand have a transplant. So we will join a very
unique club indeed. A few we already know on the ward
and it will be a comfort to share our journey with them.
The road ahead is now very different from the one we
began back in July. The chemo will continue until
Fabian is in full remission, and a further BMA on 10th
Oct will hopefully confirm this. There will be much
discussion and preparation for the transplant in the
weeks ahead involving a whole new medical team. The
Marsden is one of the UK's largest centres for
transplantation and we must constantly remind
ourselves that we are in the best possible hands. There
is now every reason to believe Fabian will be ultimately
cured. Transplant is make or break whereas chemo
only ever gives you long term remission. Those of you
who remember the film 'Deep Impact' will understand
when I say our battle against leukaemia resonates with
that story. The world faces extinction threat from a
meteor collision. A spaceship named Messiah attempts
to blow it up in space but only succeeds in splitting it
and diverting the larger of the two pieces. A last ditch

mass nuclear missile launch fails to stop the meteor. At this point the President goes on air to state, 'We hope for the best but plan for the worst'. Finally, the smaller piece hits earth and causes widespread destruction **but** extinction is averted and a remnant survives. Fabian, is and will be a survivor. He has strength of character and a living faith that is an inspiration to us.

There will be much more to tell in the days ahead and as ever, we thank you for standing with us.

FRIDAY, SEPTEMBER 30, 2011

Royal visit!

Just posting a quick update after the whirlwind events of yesterday when we all met Prince William and Catherine. Fabian appears to have become an overnight media star but is totally unfazed by all the fuss that was made of him (unlike his parents!). It will be a fantastic memory to cherish - a day of joy amid the many dark days. The royal couple were so genuine and expressed real interest and concern over his situation. If we were fans of them before we are now diehards! In case you didn't catch the media he appeared on BBC and ITV 6pm news (29th) and today's Mail, Sun and Telegraph. The FT were approached but gave no comment...

So this week of daily chemotherapy ends today and we have a euphemistically-named 'rest week' to look forward to. More anon.

FRIDAY, OCTOBER 7, 2011

Fame and reality

So, a week on from the Royal visit and we are still reminded of that wonderful day by finding Fabian has appeared in 'Hello!' and 'Ok' magazines. Folk in dentist's waiting rooms across the land will be reading his story! He is hopeful that as was reported, the Duchess will post on his guestbook, so if you are reading this Catherine, we would be honoured if you do just that!

Our 'rest' week began with a whistlestop tour of the north west and midlands to visit as many university campuses as we could. We wanted to show Oli how much colder it is up there, but untypically it was the warmest weekend for a 100 years!   The following days were then punctuated with 3 visits to the hospital for Fabian to receive the regular treatment he has to protect against the side effects of chemo. It seems ironic one needs treatment to protect against the effects of the treatment, but such is the toxicity of chemotherapy. Fabian usually fares well when at home and he has been getting stuck into some serious Lego construction as well as keeping up with school work. His latest bloodcount, though, showed he was neutropenic and as has so often been the case in the past, he duly spiked a temperature yesterday accompanied by much nausea. Lydia took him into Kingston Hospital where he remains for now receiving the ubiquitous antibiotic with which to fight the infection. His appetite always drops at these times and any chance at present of his weight recovering is no better than the economic growth forecast. So Monday's planned BMA ('spinal tap') is now uncertain. This would be a setback as our oncologist is keen to determine that he is in remission. Without this confirmation, she cannot initiate preparations for the transplant. So then, our word in faith for now is ...<u>remission</u>.

WEDNESDAY, OCTOBER 12, 2011

Fighting infection

Right then. Still incarcerated in Kingston Hospital following last Thursday's infection. The Doctors have prescribed their way through a gamut of antibiotics, each one not yet managing to stabilise his spiking temperature, and CRP cell markers remain detectable. A chest X ray and ultrasound haven't revealed anything insidious such as the odd fungal spot or two. Fabian himself appears to be clinically well and some of his appetite has bounced back. He is a bit more fussy about the food here which is not quite up to the a la carte choice and gastronomical standards of the Marsden. Obviously the next BMA and stage of chemo is put back until his temperature stabilises and neutrophil count rises *(could somebody develop an app that works out the probability of an oncology procedure keeping to schedule?).* I'll post again once I have confirmation of Fabian's next move.
Welcome to any new subscribers who recently received the Faith4Fabian bookmark. Do say Hi via the Guestbook!

SATURDAY, OCTOBER 15, 2011

A royal surprise

It's 7am on a chill October morning. Our cockerel is punctuating the still air with metronomic 'cock-a-doodle-do's'. I've just peeked in Fabian's bedroom to remind myself that, yes, he really is back home in his own bed (next to Cassia who offered to be his hot water bottle last night). He was given the all clear at 9am yesterday but in NHS terms that means a 4 hour delay by the time all the discharge routines, drug prescriptions and final obs are done. It is good to see him in such high spirits again, keen to pick up the Lego construction he left off 8 days ago. We managed a quick jaunt over to Legoland especially as the weather was glorious. There was, however, a very timely surprise awaiting him - a personal letter, sent special delivery complete with Buckingham Palace postmark, from the Duchess of Cambridge (or Kate as we have come to know her!). As this is, of course in the national interest, we've shared it with you via the Photo section without any redactions..We are very honoured that she has made this gesture for our Fabian. We know it doesn't change the reality of his situation but it gives us a tremendous feel-good factor and is a positive distraction from the weariness of this fight against leukaemia. A certain royal reporter has shown special interest in our story so there may yet be more to share. So the next few days will be spent at home before the delayed bone marrow aspirate on Tuesday. Thereafter Fabian is to be admitted on Thursday for a long stretch of treatment (cytarobine and aspariginase - the Brothers Grimm). A practical complication next week is that Lydia herself requires some routine diagnostic surgery on her throat so some meticulous planning and logistics is going to be needed. I suspect our half term break is going to be anything but.

Fabian has been watching the visitor counter to the blog rise steadily and is always glad to see a new guestbook entry, growing with international contributions (welcome USA, NZ). Your encouragements are recorded for him forever and form an ongoing petition to God for his total healing and cure (Phil 4:6). Thank you!

TUESDAY, OCTOBER 18, 2011

Media spotlight and normality

I'm blogging this from secret central London location, well a top-notch hotel overlooking the London Eye. We are here at the invitation (and expense!) of Daybreak, ITV's breakfast show. It's the culmination of a white-knuckle ride during the past 48 hours all triggered by that amazing letter from Kate to Fabian. Press and media have shown an insatiable demand for this story and it's particularly gratifying that the work of the children's unit at the Marsden gets recognition from this exposure. And yet life and treatment for Fabian continues as per norm. Today we were back on the unit for his BMA which went without complication although once again a sample was problematic and they took instead a trephine (core of hip bone) which has left him a bit sore, as you'd expect! The result, fateful or otherwise is expected by Thursday, the day on which he will be admitted as an inpatient once again. So we will thoroughly enjoy tomorrow. Do catch the live show if you can or on ITV Player at your leisure. I'm off for a jacuzzi.

SATURDAY, OCTOBER 22, 2011

Fame and chemo

Andy Warhol once said; *"In the future, everyone will be famous for 15 minutes"*. On that basis, my family has already expended their allotted time! He later changed his mind and declared; *"In 15 minutes, everyone will be famous"*, which if you consider the speed at which news is disseminated around the globe via all manner of media, is now a reality. We certainly have found in the last week how a moving story and a royal touch has appealed to such a wide audience. It's humbling to consider that Fabian, amongst so many other cancer children should be the focus. He's handled it brilliantly, endearing himself to all those he met. Particularly charming was King of Cool, Henry Winkler who pronounced; "Fabian, my hero!" on live TV. Some, of course, may question our agreement to such media exposure for him when he himself cannot consent. But our belief is that this has happened for such a time as this and God means it for good - too much bad has happened for us not to think otherwise. Heart-warming for us too, to read the hundreds of Internet comments of support posted online for Fabian's continued strength and a positive outcome. I'm sure we will reread these as we go through transplant.

So now we continue our journey of treatment with Fabian back at the Marsden receiving daily doses of cytarabin, dexamethasone and aspariginase with a splash of cotrixamole on the side. Initially he's bearing up well to this toxic onslaught. I hesitate to sound more convincing.. Strangely we have not had the bone marrow result which suggests there is nothing of concern or simply that one doctor thinks another has already told us. This happened before. Lydia's own surgery has been put back to next week after some intense inter-NHS wrangling between surgeons' secretaries. This decision is surely for the better. It will take place at the sister Marsden hospital in Fulham so I shall hold the unique accolade of having a member of my family admitted to both Marsden's at the same time. National insurance value indeed!

Be with you again soon.

WEDNESDAY, OCTOBER 26, 2011

Hospital and drugs

I'm here at Kingston Hospital where Fabian is having his regular ambisone infusion. Being treated like a royal by the nurses is going down well with him; food, drink, DVDs – all are provided at his request! We were surprised by his unexpected discharge from the Marsden on Monday night. He'd remained so well throughout the first course of cytarabine he's been allowed home in between blocks, the next one beginning tomorrow. He's back on the ward now, rather than in isolation and I'd forgotten how disruptive that can be to a night's sleep when I stayed last weekend. Intermittent beeping from intravenous pumps, crying babies, lights on and off are just some examples. The new £18 million Children's unit is now fully operational and we could not be in a more state of the art centre. We heard today the provisional date for Fabian's transplant – 8th December – T Day. His latest marrow results are still incomplete and depending on the morphology test, he may be required to have an additional intensive chemo block that would push that date back by a month. I'm guessing though, that Christmas will be spent in isolation. I only hope Santa scrubs up before permeating the lead-lined walls of the radiation suite. Lyd's own operation takes place in the morning so it goes without saying she would value your thoughts and prayers. A steady stream of prepared meals given by friends means we have a well-stocked freezer to see us through a week without Mum's cooking. To those of you enjoying a half term break, tell me what it feels like! Dieu et mon droit.

OCTOBER 28, 2011

A day to remember

This blog has always been focused on Fabian's journey, but I'll also cover other family matters and today, that is to tell you about Lydia's surgery. I have to confess the last 48 hours have been entirely forgettable – and I wasn't the one having surgery! We had a 6.30am start on the day of her operation to check in to preadmission at the Royal Marsden, Fulham, a rather imposing building, set incongruously amongst the fashion shops of Chelsea. We had a brief discussion with the surgical team about the procedure before Lydia donned the somewhat unfashionable theatre gown (one size fits all!) and did her make-up (no, not really). The op was planned for early afternoon so I hot-footed back home in order to collect Fabian where he was due to be at the sister hospital in Sutton. This entirely confused my satnav, not knowing which Marsden destination applied. There was the usual welcome for him on arrival; cook Jacquie with the menu, nurse Tania to do the obs and a doctor looking important. Oli had agreed (coerced!) to be on duty and I was able to head back to Chelsea, hoping not to miss Lydia coming out of recovery. However, she was held there a few hours longer than anticipated so I got a parking ticket instead. Those of you who have undergone a full anaesthetic and surgery will be only too aware that one never looks one's best immediately post-op. Still, it was very upsetting to see my dearest in such a poorly condition and my usual stoicism somewhat failed me. The operation though had gone as well as expected and the Sweeney Todd-sized gash she had feared was thankfully a small(ish) incision which we are assured will blend in with the natural skin folds. Results of the biopsy are due in a week and we remain confident this will prove to be benign. That night for her on the ward could best be described as a 'Night at the Museum' with all the groans, cries and comings and going. Thankfully, the doctors gave the all-clear today so half the family are now back at home, figuring out the care rota for next week. Apparently I still have a job to do, and even a looming Ofsted inspection of my college for which I must prepare. Thank you to the many who have sent us messages of encouragement at this time. "Those who are for us are greater than those who are against us".

Results day!

We've had to face a number of medical results over the last 5 years, most of them bad – the initial diagnosis, the positive MRD meaning higher risk category, the relapse and the failure to reach remission. But this week we can celebrate two results that have been a huge relief. Firstly, the final tests on Fabian's recent aspirate confirmed he is in a sufficient state of remission to avoid an additional, heavy block of chemo and he remains on track for transplant in December. This will also give him more time at home beforehand which as you know by now is always preferable. Secondly and thankfully, the result of Lydia's thyroid lumpectomy has proved it was benign and she has been given the-all clear. This of course is wonderful news, but the sheer relief that there was at least no further cancer in the family brought us both to tears and no doubt perplexed the surgeon who was probably expecting a 'hi-five'. I think the emotional strain of the past few months, with its highs and lows is catching up with us, but a decent cappuccino and prayer of thanks afterwards and our batteries feel recharged. So back to Fabian, still in the Marsden after having completed the intensification block of treatment but not clinically well enough to go home. He has endured a terrible irritation around his eyes due to an eye drop that was needed to counteract a known side effect. That has now subsided but his neutrophils are south of 0.1 and he's needed two blood transfusions in the past 72 hours. Nowadays, the ward is busier with a seeming conveyor belt of children at various stages of transplant. One dear lady has just emerged with her son after 42 days in isolation. Her recommendation to us was, 'buy your own fridge!'. Tomorrow the children have a bonfire night party but without fireworks or a bonfire. A crudely-made 'guy' sits in the corridor, resplendent in doctors' coat and surgical gloves. Ben turns 15 on Saturday. It'll be one of the first birthdays when we have not all been together as a family as I don't think he's convinced about spending his day at the hospital! Despite present demands, we also have to think and plan for Fabian's future, in particular his education during periods at home. I'm appalled to date at how problematic and bureaucratic the process has been to secure one to one tuition for him which he is entitled to by virtue of his medical condition. A great deal of tenacity and patience is needed – don't they know that Fabian has royal backing?? And ladies, get your copy of 'Woman's Own' this week to see our superhero in print.

NOVEMBER 12, 2011

Blood counts down but not out

I usually wait until there is some exciting news to blog. But a week has passed and very little has happened. The slow wait for Fabian's blood counts to rise seems inexorable. Seven straight days with zero neutrophils and then a teasing glimmer of hope when it rose to 0.1 only to fall back again the following day. This outcome after a heavy course of cytarabine was always predicted (doctors can be so right sometimes) but we are thankful that Fabian has remained so well throughout, although at the time of writing he has just spiked a couple of temperatures so the ubiquitous antibiotics are back on stream. In the main, Lydia stays with Fabian whilst I am back at work having the hard life!! It hardly seems two weeks since her own operation and she is recovering well but will probably have to bring the '70's choker back into fashion until her scar heals. Family separation for many days, and now weeks presents its own challenges, compounded recently by the fact that the WiFi was down in the ward rendering skype communication inoperable (and the mobile signal is pitiful). Preparations for the transplant are underway in terms of us meeting the team and specialist nurses to discuss the procedure. A more colourful description though, can be gained from meeting other parents in the kitchen… The transplant date has predictably changed – now much closer to Christmas. What joy! We've passed a milestone this month with the 500th visit to this site which is testament to your continued faithfulness (and tenacity!). Still, Fabian's US friend Riley is closer to 10,000 visits, so we have a way to go!!

NOVEMBER 17, 2011

Doldrums and discussion

I'm tempted to put "ditto" for today's entry. Not much has changed since the last one. Fabian's blood counts remain doggedly in the doldrums, much like the economic forecast. I wish it were Robert Peston announcing the results; *'So, we've seen a staggering increase of one trillion neutrophils'*. Alas, then there is no immediate prospect of his homecoming but Fabian is showing fighting spirit. He's had more celebrity encounters in the last week; comedian Tim Vine dropped by as did Fearne Cotton whom he described as 'that woman on TV'. We've had the first formal discussion with the transplant team which was both scary and reassuring. The sheer volume of information to take on board is awesome. The NHS call it patient empowerment – and apparently we are now fully informed and able to give consent. To be fair, Lydia and I had both done our homework in preparation for this and were not as over-awed as might have been the case. It was Marie Curie who said; 'nothing is to be feared, only understood' and I agree knowledge is a good antidote to facing the unknown. But then another well-known person, Jesus, said; 'do not be afraid, only believe'. Oleander, too has had her health checks and briefing about what she will undergo as Fabian's donor. It's no small undertaking for a 17-year-old and she is handling it all herself in a very mature way which makes us proud. At this stage their preference is to use her since harvesting stem cells is easier and more productive with an older sibling. There may even be some spare for the Anthony Nolan bank! We do now know that she is CMV-ve whereas Fabian is CMV+ve which means that he carries a common virus which Oli does not and so will be at risk of catching the very infection post-transplant that he currently has immunity against! There is a strange irony about this, but in such an event there would be ample treatment to deal with it. We are naturally most anxious about the total body irradiation (TBI) that is given during conditioning. This, as you would expect, causes the worst side effects but in the States, their leading transplantation unit no longer uses TBI and has shown improved cure rates. Over here it is still the norm and we would be ill-advised to question this. But we are quietly confident by the 3 positives in Fabian's favour – a perfect sibling donor, good tolerance of treatment to date, age and clinical state (sorry, that's 4 positives!).

NOVEMBER 26, 2011

Homeward bound

Finally, expectation met reality yesterday and Fabian has been discharged from Bed 2, his home for the past 28 days. I am pleased to say this coincided neatly with the fact that I had arrived on Friday to relieve Lydia and take the weekend stint. Life can be so fair sometimes! Having carefully packed up his 'LegoCity', I promptly tripped outside with the box and shattered 1,274 pieces across the car park. Groan. Fabian, of course is very happy to be back home if somewhat skeptical that it is for more than a day or two. He and Lydia have had the privilege to get to know a diverse range of families in the past weeks, all of whom share the common bond of coping with childhood cancer. There is incredible fortitude in this community in the face of desperate odds. Emotions are never far from the surface but there is always someone, it would seem in a worse predicament than yourself and at such times one can be a comfort. The nursing staff exemplify some of the best in the care sector. They've needed a good sense of humour, especially when caring for Fabian!

So the facts are; he has completed a further chemo block (methotrexate) and apart from a brief return of diarrhoea has remained well and free of infection. There is now no further chemo due before he begins conditioning pre-transplant. Monday's bone marrow aspirate has confirmed he is in a state of full remission (amen!) but we still await his MRD, that critical molecular result which will tell us the *actual* level of remission (less than 1 leukaemic cell per million is some kind of threshold). We are believing this will be the case so that he can remain on track for BMT just before Christmas. Keeping him well for the next few weeks is the name of the game. Any spike in temperature could mean a return to Bed 2 (or wherever) so our house is declared a bug-free zone. We have a series of appointments with transplant, radiography and ultrasound teams ahead so a normal family routine will remain elusive, but then it will do until we finally kick this leukaemia into touch. Thankfully we have managed to share Cassia's 12th birthday together and a 'pamper' party is arranged for her tonight (er, not the boys though). Oli has taken a small step closer to reaching medical school having been offered 2 interviews to date. No small feat considering the massive oversubscription for places. I'm sure donating her stem cells next month is the best preparation she could ever have to becoming a doctor and helping save life.

If you're reading this blog for the first time, welcome and do post us a comment!

DECEMBER 2, 2011

Remission – how sweet the sound!

So, a week on already since his discharge. Life seems a lot busier when we're all at home. No that it's entirely a bed of roses for Fabian. He's had a nasty bout of mouth ulcers and cracked lips. If you've ever had a mild ulcer, you know how painful they can be and bonjela offered him less relief than drinking copious amounts of Coke which seemed to numb the pain until we got a proper prescription. As with all these side effects, they come and go and we have found yet another type of pain relief. But the good, nay great news this week has been the lab result of his MRD which is negative. This confirms he is in total remission (no more than one in a million leukaemic cells!) and will be spared the additional heavy chemo block that would have also postponed transplant. But equally, it raises the question for us as to whether chemo alone could still provide a cure? We had never expected to be heading to transplant as Fabian was classified a late relapse and the normal protocol for this scenario would preclude a transplant. And yet following the relapse he unfortunately did not go into remission 'as quickly' as he should have, hence the doctor's belief that only transplant can cure his leukaemia. However, the earlier MRD samples, as our readers may recall, were poor (based on a trephine, not marrow) and perhaps not a totally reliable source on which to base such a profound decision. As the time for transplant consent draws close, we therefore feel an awesome responsibility to choose the right path for Fabian. Our fact-finding and research to help us in this has been extensive and we are grateful to friends who have assisted us in this. Today we met the radiographer, a disarming man with a dry wit who gave a forthright presentation of the horrendous potential side effects the use of total body irradiation (TBI) might have. Not for the faint-hearted, or indeed the stout-hearted. There were many we had not fully contemplated; secondary malignancies, impaired lung function, loss of endocrine control, vascular problems, cataracts, cognitive impairment, pneumonitis, spleen infection and these in addition to infertility. Signing the consent for TBI afterward was akin to agreeing to send your son to Chernobyl. Again, there is an alternative, more widely used in the States – busulphan (a chemo drug) instead of TBI. But the message was clear; TBI is best. Fabian will now go for a full body CT scan on Monday as a precursor to TBI and the countdown to the so-called 'Day Zero' has begun. There was a happy moment for Fabian on the way home as he was able to pop into his school briefly and see old chums. They really miss him and he knows he is very much loved by those in the school community. To keep the connection, we've had fun experimenting with skype to create a virtual link with his class. although nothing can quite replace face to face. So with Christmas in hospital a certainty, Fabian's been asking for a Christmas tree so we've decided to decorate early and create a festive environment before he has to leave. Those of you praying, please ask for wisdom for us. Our thanks and love.

DECEMBER 9, 2011

Scent of Christmas

A busy week and one that has been strangely devoid of medical complications. Our fighter, Fabian is resurgent in remission and has regained much of his energy, appetite and mischief. He's even able to have home tutor visits during this time. We're generally keeping him indoors and away from public areas due to the proliferation of coughs and colds at this time of year. The direst thing to happen right now would be an infection that could delay transplant – Day Zero. Now let me tell you more about Day Zero. I make an analogy with Ground Zero; (1) his bone marrow (the Twin Towers) having been attacked by leukemia (terrorism) needs to be totally destroyed by a powerful dose of chemo and total body irradiation. (2) Stem cells donated by his sister generate an entirely new bone marrow (the Freedom Tower) which grows in its place, healthier and stronger. Furthermore, this has an 'anti-leukaemic' effect for the rest of Fabian's life although the flip side to this advantage is the new immunity may well also treat his healthy cells as foreign and cause the so-called graft versus host disease...for the rest of his life. It's as simple as that, well not quite. Having spent another couple of hours this week with the transplant team going over the finer detail, we now have all the facts and fully acknowledge this is his best chance of healing. People ask us about the cure rates for allogeneic (sibling match) transplant. Despite working with data in my day job, I steer clear of studying the morbidity stats but suffice to say, if this was an investment choice it would make the euro look secure and the health warnings would not be out of place on a cigarette pack. But our faith, though shaken, remains firm and Fabian's spirit is testament to God's Hand on his life. So we have signed the consent form and now have one further week at home before his admission next Friday. The tree is up and the Christmas cake baked; the scent of cinnamon evokes the festive season, that is, until Ben's prolific use of deodorant snuffs it out. Teenagers!

DECEMBER 15, 2011

Setback

We've had disappointing news; the transplant is to be delayed.

Following her medical assessment, Oleander can no longer donate her stem cells. Cassia (12), amazingly, must now step in and take her place, albeit this also means the procedure will not go ahead until after the New Year. It's an awesome responsibility on her young shoulders. I think we will keep her wrapped in cotton wool until that time! Nevertheless, we are terribly frustrated at this setback and Oli is naturally upset. Our immediate plans (foolish to even make any!) have dissolved but we now at least have Christmas together at home for which Fabian is most pleased. That's not to say he will avoid further hospital trips. The delay means he'll require a 'top up' chemo block in order to maintain remission so more vinchristine, methotrexate and mercaptopurine with a dash of steroids. Yes, it would have been lovely for Fabian to start 2012 with a new immune system but perhaps this was not meant to be and the whole episode reminds us how little we can trust what is seen and how much we must trust by faith in what is unseen. '*For I know the plans I have for you, plans to give you hope and a future*' Jer 29:11

DECEMBER 25, 2011

Thankful this Christmas

I must admit to overdoing the sentimentality at Christmas time. It's an occasion that endures through the generations and childhood memories flood back when seeing one's own children enjoying the festivities. Obviously, this year holds special importance. We are so thankful to have Fabian unexpectedly at home and in such good health and it's difficult to imagine what he will face in a few short weeks. For now, it's just a pleasure to see him with Ben, Cassia and Oleander knee deep in discarded wrapping paper jostling for supremacy in the 'best present' stakes. This year, a cash gift has emerged as the clear winner! We've had a busy week leading up to Christmas with visits to daycare for the maintenance chemo block which includes the mood-swinging steroid dexamethasone. Hence there have been a fair few cases of temper tantrums induced by the slightest infringement of his familial rights (though not exactly a new phenomenon!). We did manage a trip to the Hampton Court ice rink but Fabian was confined to watching from the side since the risk of falling over whilst having an implanted Hickman line was too great. Chicken catching in the garden however, was fine!

Our next key hospital date is January 5th when we take Cassia for screening and further checks on Fabian. Due to her age and size, she will need a more intrusive procedure to harvest the stem cells direct from the bone marrow in her hip. Fabian was a bit concerned about the change in donor as when told he queried , 'but Oli has more blood'. In reality, the chances of success with either sister are equal although we do know that research suggests less long term chronic GvHD when using bone marrow rather than peripheral blood so the 'setback' may well benefit Fabian in the long run. As always, much to know and understand and I am ever conscious of being an informed amateur in these matters. So to end this entry, Lydia and I would like to thank all our followers across the world for their interest in faith4fabian and the many who send their prayers and encouragement without which this would often be a lonely place indeed. We wish you and yours and truly wonderful Christmas. *'Have faith in Him who he has sent'* John 6:29

JANUARY 5, 2012 |

New year, new plan

Well, we are now referring to Fabian's relapse as being *last* year. Hard to believe it is nearly 6 months since that woeful day in July. After a homely but lackadaisical Christmas and New Year during which Fabian piled on the pounds, we had a very hectic time at the Marsden today with no less than 3 individual consultant appointments, multiple blood tests and an ECG. This is all in connection with Plan B (or was it always Plan A?) to now use Cassia as Fabian's donor. One of the interviews was regarding the Human Tissue Authority Guidelines to ensure 'no coercement or undue reward is being made to the donor'. Not sure if tickets to see a certain well-known boy band fall foul of this in Cassia's case.. So the perceived wisdom is to proceed as soon as possible to transplant which carries more certainty of happening with her rather than Oli. In turns out there may be a better prognosis and less side effects using stem cells harvested from the marrow in a younger child so it feels like there is a silver lining to all this. We have also requested a further bone marrow aspirate to confirm he has remained in full remission, which as you recall was our main concern when we learnt of the postponement. So dates are set for Fabian to be admitted later this month with the transplant proceeding the following week (caveat: all NHS plans are subject to change!). Having made such a weight gain will stand him in good stead in the weeks ahead. Even his hair has begun to grow back and together with Ben, who more or less shaved his head recently, we have a couple of skinheads at home! I forgot to mention in the last post that we had received a further royal letter, this time from Duchess Kate's private secretary, wishing us well with the forthcoming transplant. Although unknowingly premature, it was heartening that she had obviously diarised this event and taken the trouble to follow up. Her interest will always remain a huge encouragement to us, as indeed do your ongoing prayers.

JANUARY 20, 2012

The day after tomorrow

Ask Fabian whether he still needs a bone marrow transplant and he'll point to the fact that his hair is growing back so he must be better. And he has been extremely well of late, great appetite, loads of energy and even a spate of heavy night sweats had completely stopped after praying against this symptom. We know too, he is still in full remission following test results from the bone marrow aspirate last week. So it's with a strange reluctance that he and Lydia must return today to the Marsden to commence conditioning treatment for the planned procedure next Friday. We constantly remind ourselves of the 'miracle' that he has the choice of 2 sibling donors which is to us a sign of God's abundance in his healing, giving him a choice of 100% matches when so many families struggle to find even one. For sure, it's going to be hard watching the radiation treatment and the hugely toxic cyclophosphamide infusions start the day after tomorrow and I only hope we can show the same mental toughness that Fabian has. Cassia is all set to play her crucial part, although all encouragement to make her eat more iron-boosting greens has failed! I'll update more frequently now that things are rolling so do remember to subscribe to the (new) post alert via the link below the visitor map. God bless you all, onwards and upwards.

JANUARY 24, 2012

One Direction – no turning back

Do bloggers ever get writers block? It's cold and dark outside and I'm struggling to find an inspired start to this entry. Maybe that was it? So to tell you what's been happening; we are already well into the conditioning treatment which is medically speaking 'going well' but emotionally tough on us. Our wonderful Fabian is being so brave and compliant with this. Yesterday I took him into one of the irradiation sessions where he dutifully laid out on the highly uncomfortable positioning bed in the so-called mould room. The radiation beam gun, technically called a Linear Accelerator, would not look out of place in a Star Wars movie – and it's huge. Think dentist's X-ray gun times 20. Once the beam's cross hairs are aligned, we all leave decant to the NASA-style control room where we can monitor him via CCTV. This is one TV set I would rather not see him on. And he has to remain perfectly still for half an hour or so which he has done so well. Afterwards, the nurse awards him with stickers and he gets some 'courage beads' that glow in the dark (as indeed he probably will!). There have been some early side effects including headaches, nausea and vomiting but Fabian has kept in high spirits. We've been given a spacious and comfortable room which is home for the next few weeks and already resembles a Lego building site now that he's settled in. Cassia will join him and Lydia later in the week. Now that treatment to destroy Fabian's immunity has begun, there is no turning back and she is, quite simply, his lifeline so one is understandably nervous about her doing anything that might be remotely hazardous! That said, she had the shock treat of her life at the weekend when she was invited to join a select few children to meet the boy band 'One Direction'. I had approached the band's management a while back asking for this favour but had heard nothing until a couple of days ago when I was called by the charity Rays of Sunshine who had been passed our details by them. By amazing coincidence, the boys were performing at Hammersmith that weekend so were able to schedule in this meet and greet with perfect timing. Now if you're not 12 and female you may not understand what the fuss is all about but believe me it was on a par with meeting William and Kate for her! I only hope the adrenalin rush to her blood has calmed down in time for the transplant. Check out the pics in the gallery. So I close this, reminded of our abundant God who produces water from rock and makes a desert place fertile. Thank you for what we know has been a surge in prayers and petitions for Fabian this week.

JANUARY 25, 2012

Conditioning and make up

We're now well past the halfway mark for transplant conditioning. Six down, two TBI sessions to go. There was a brief hiatus at this afternoon's session when the accelerator broke down and Fabian was left in limbo whilst they hastily transferred everything over to the backup unit. The initial novelty of this treatment has well and truly worn off and coupled with the increasing fatigue it causes, he is now very reluctant to head off to radiography when the nurse calls. His white blood count is already down to 0.2 thus nearing zero immunity, so the zapping is doing its work. Cassia is now admitted so Fabian will be cheered up by having his sister's company. Meanwhile, she is rather concerned about what to wear for tomorrow's op; next, next she'll be wanting to go into hair and make-up (in jest)! Obviously, as we draw near to Day Zero there is little else on our minds, so if there's a global catastrophe in the meantime, could someone post a comment in case we miss it? Or just leave a comment anyway, especially our international followers. We appreciate you.

JANUARY 27, 2012 |

Day Zero

So, transplant day arrived! Somewhat of an anti-climax given that the procedure is in effect merely a mega blood transfusion. I still wonder how they can squeeze an additional pint of blood into a child's body, albeit Fabian looked very rosy-cheeked afterward, whereas poor Cassia looks very peaky. She though, was well enough to come home today, armed with 3 months' supply of iron supplement. At last then, with the start of a brand new immune system, we can say for certainty our 6 year battle against leukaemia has turned the corner and that in the great words of Churchill spoken in 1942, "Now this is not the end. It is not even the beginning of the end. But it is, perhaps, the end of the beginning" (pardon the melodramatic). The key weapon Fabian now has is the Graft vs Leukaemia effect (GvL) meaning that his new lymphocytes are locked and loaded, set to attack and destroy any remaining leukaemic cells. Of course, there is a long uncertain road ahead and first to face will be the small matter of engraftment. We need the new stem cells to engraft in Fabian and the first sign of this will be an increase in his WBC count. The magic number 0.5 will indicate this has happened so everyone repeat after me; 'Grow cells grow'. I know this works because a 4 year old leukaemia child in America tried this on followers of his blog and he raced to engraftment. Tonight the room is properly sealed up to ward off infection and Lydia will hunker down with Fabian, regularly peered at by staff through the door slats. More news anon.

FEBRUARY 3, 2012

Days of Zero

D+7: one week today since transplant. Not much of interest to report whilst we await engraftment; rather like watching paint dry. The first tell-tale signs of GvHD have appeared; mucositis, diarrhoea and skin rash. This is exactly as predicted and is actually a good sign (not if you ask Fabian!). As they say in post-transplant circles, 'a little bit of GvHD does you good'. The frustrating effect of this is complete loss of appetite and as a result he had to endure (again) the ignominy of a nasal gastric tube inserted so that nutrition can be supplied on demand. Whilst on the positive side, at least his hair continues to grow back. Each day we get the blood counts – and each day its zero. So remember the chant – 'grow cells grow'. Isolation is very boring. There are only so many Lego permutations one can build. The photo below illustrates Fabian's latest construction. I caught an item on ITV's Daybreak this week which featured a little boy who has come through bone marrow transplant, thanks only to a last-minute donor being found on the Anthony Nolan bank following an appeal on the programme last year. We are ever grateful that our circumstances were so much more straightforward. We were also reminded by a catholic friend that the day of his transplant was in fact the feast of St Fabian, a first century Pope. Totally unplanned of course, but maybe a spiritual sign, none the less?

FEBRUARY 8, 2012

Whose perspective?

D+12: No flicker of movement on the blood 'countometer'. In fact, Fabian's platelets fell to single figures requiring a further transfusion. The mucositis has well and truly taken hold and necessitated intravenous morphine for pain relief which Fabian controls with a pulse button. He only needs this intermittently but perversely, morphine can exacerbate the side effects itself. His thickening hair is in fact falling out again (ho hum) and is now a rather monk-like style. Eating continues to be negligible therefore the nasogastric tube remains in regular use, so with all the various fluid connections, Fabian is limited to a six-foot radius of movement. He has been continuing his learning with the teaching staff and is very proud of his work. We've tried skyping his class during lessons but this proved more of a welcome distraction to the other pupils! He enjoys visits from his brother and sisters, even if this is limited to gesturing through the glass. Despite his obvious medical condition, the doctors seem very pleased with his progress so I guess it's a question of perspective – and they have seen far worse cases than him at this stage. So we do believe the prayer surrounding Fabian is sustaining and protecting him from more acute reactions. A date for your diary – March 2nd will be his 10th birthday and it would be truly wonderful to have everyone home for that occasion. Let's believe for it!

FEBRUARY 12, 2012

A flicker..

D+16: When Elijah saw a cloud the size of a man's fist in the distance, it was the first sign of the downpour to come. So it is for Fabian, as a flicker in his counts yesterday indicated the presence of fledgling white blood cells and a rise in neutrophils. Cells have grown! This was rather short-lived as it has fallen back again to zero but nevertheless the doctors who "aren't promising anything" say it looks positive. He's continuing to struggle with frequent vomiting, mild temperatures and general lethargy. Today he needed yet another platelet transfusion as well as red blood. One wonders how the body can accommodate such increases in fluids. He recently told me his wish was "to be myself again" which everyone, I know, will be hoping for him. Lydia has gone home for a couple of days to recharge and will no doubt miss the cleanliness and order of Room 9! Her 24/7 dedication to caring for Fabian is unstinting. It's half term and the children are home, glad of the chance to lie-in especially on these cold mornings. We're probably at the mid-point of Fabian's time in isolation. It's felt like a time warp in which the world is passing by whilst we are in groundhog day. All downhill now..

Half empty

D+ 22: I've always tried to write this blog through a 'half full' perspective; no-one wants to read a 'woe is me' diarist. But there are times when feeling 'half empty' would be telling it as it is and this week fits that bill nicely. As noted last time, Fabian's WBC has started to rise and we think engraftment is not too far off, especially as he is now 22 days post-transplant. Other than that, his health has not been good and it is thoroughly soul-destroying to see him struggling with the raft of side effects on a constant basis. A recent complication has been a chest infection which may or may not be viral but which they are attacking with an armoury of antibiotics. This toxic onslaught caused his kidney function to deteriorate so they have had to pull back the dosage to allow this to recover. The mucositis, itching, vomiting, diarrhoea and lethargy all persist and Fabian expelled his NG tube a few days ago (again) so lack of nutrition is back on the agenda. He is understandably a lot grumpier these days and visits are not exactly a pleasant exchange of well-wishing! We're both still immensely proud of his resilience and fortitude and these qualities will help him overcome much in later life. Other family issues are not helping to make life a bed of roses at present but I'd like to end on a half full thought, reminding myself that 'He who is in us is greater than he who is in the world'. Join me next time for better news!

FEBRUARY 20, 2012

And here is the better news..

D+24: I ended my last entry promising to bring better news next time and for once my expectations have been surpassed. Fabian's blood counts have leapt massively in the past 48 hours and today, for the first time since transplant, they lifted the isolation restrictions and 'opened' the door. So to quote Braveheart, "FREEDOM!". But 4 weeks in room 9 has so conditioned Fabian to live with captivity he was reluctant to step outside and even felt rather down about the possibility. I'm sure this will pass. So was this sudden change in fortune a miracle I hear the prayer warriors ask? Well, not exactly.. For the past few days he has been on Granulocyte Colony Stimulating Factor, known as GCSF. This is often given where engraftment is slow and is rather like jump-starting a car whose battery is too flat to start itself. The GCSF stimulates stem cell production and in Fabian's case it has certainly done the trick. The commensurate rise in neutrophils has also helped clear the infection and bring down his temperatures and some of his energy has returned, enough to resume construction of Lego project that had been shelved. He's even started to eat small amounts of solids and managed to hold it down. Such a different Fabian from the one a few short days ago; we're truly thankful to God. It's likely his counts will fall back slightly once they stop the GCSF and they need to see them remain for at least 3 consecutive days above the threshold before declaring he has properly engrafted. The flipside of engrafting is an increase in GvHD which in Fabian's case is a nasty rash so he's now on steroids which will combat that side effect.

Now what was that about feeling half empty?

FEBRUARY 25, 2012

But here is the best news!

They say a week in politics is a long time. But nothing compared to a week in oncology. Only 7 days ago Fabian had blood counts near zero, was eating nothing and still suffering an infection with high temperatures. By yesterday, his counts had risen more than tenfold, he was clear of all infection and stabilised and tucking into fried rice. So... they've allowed him home temporarily! There was little notice of this decision and even after letting Lyd know, the doctors ordered one more platelet transfusion to see him on his way. But <u>pure joy</u> to see him come through the door last night and an epiphany moment for me to grasp that by the grace of God and the wonders of medicine, our little boy has come through a major high-risk procedure relatively unscathed. At some point in the week, he technically achieved engraftment which means his new stem cells (Cassia's old ones!) are now firing on all cylinders generating lymphocytes and neutrophils which will gradually replace his immune system over the next 6 months. This was no foregone conclusion. We know of 2 other children on the ward who sadly passed away following complications post-transplant and Fabian himself was seriously at risk during the peak of his chest infection, although this was understated at the time. This homecoming is more of a parole since Fabian will be closely monitored for a while to come and indeed will be back in hospital tomorrow for bloods and meds. In fact, Lydia was handed a sackful of medicine which we'll need to administer at home and I thought for interest I'd give you a run down; cyclosporine, prednisolone, lansoprazole, itraconazole, aciclovir and phenooxymethylpenicillin for starters – who said Latin was dead? For now, we'll enjoy the moment and take each day as it comes as we have had to do for the past 214 days since Fabian relapsed. This uplifting Ron Kenoly track sums it up: **<u>He's Been Good</u>**

MARCH 2, 2012

Poignant celebration

Today we are celebrating Fabian's 10th birthday! He is
elated to have finally reached double figures and
considering what he has had to face in his short life we
certainly share that feeling. It was made especially
happy as he has been allowed home today to be with
close family and friends who came to share the day with
him, although not before he met yet another celebrity
visitor to the Children's Unit, namely England Rugby
captain Chris Robshaw together with girlfriend, Camila
Kerslake <u>LINK</u> . Unfortunately, Fabian was a little too
frank by stating that he 'didn't like rugby' which made
the 6'2″ 17st man cry (er no, not really). The week to
date has been rather stop start because of fluctuations
in his vital signs which have needed close monitoring in
hospital. The immune suppressants and steroids both
reduce GvHd but cause high blood pressure and his
renal function is creaking under the weight of so much
toxin. In fact, Fabian's own immunity could still reject
the donor cells so it is important to keep it suppressed
and this frustratingly means he's not allowed food
supplements or vitamins that would help build up his
health. We have been briefed about the conditions for
his hospital discharge (hopefully tomorrow) and these
require a strict regime at home to keep him protected
from infection. So no more chicken catching for a
while!

On a more poignant note, we were very saddened to
learn of the deaths of a further two children whom we
knew. Both were on the ward where we met William
and Kate and it is truly sobering to think that despite
the best possible medical intervention, this cancer has

claimed two more promising lives. The Royals themselves have expressed their sorrow at the news although this was a press story probably no-one wanted. So, a birthday and a forthcoming discharge; two more milestones along the path to total healing and the road seems a little less travelled.

MARCH 10, 2012

Groundhog Day

I expect one of your worst nightmares is to be stuck in a time-warp where the same day's activities continually repeat themselves, as depicted in the film of the above name. So it has been for Fabian and Lydia this past week as each day has brought the same cycle of spiking temperatures and fluctuating blood pressure – first up, then down, then up again. The doctors follow a well-worn path of medication to deal with this but it is apparently quite normal at this stage post-transplant for the body to react this way until the new immune system has taken hold. Our 'friend' GvHD is back with its accompanying itchy all-over rash that is quite uncomfortable for Fabian, stuck in bed with not much to distract him (no space for Lego City now, sadly). Having been moved from the isolation suite we are now back on the ward which has become so familiar over time. I mentally noted that at some point or other, Fabian has spent time in every one of its beds. So our discharge from hospital remains on hold but each day is surely one step closer. Tomorrow is the Great Marsden March when hundreds will walk the 14 miles between the two Marsden hospitals for charity. Having had both my wife and son treated by them, I can honestly say they are institutions worthy of support. I'll be taking part in a similar type event myself next month so if you are able, do sponsor me. Thanks for reading!

MARCH 18, 2012

That was the week that was

Alas, a very forgettable week. We have all been hit to varying degrees with the 'flu and for the past 4 days remained holed up indoors recovering from this wretched virus. Even our GP had to make a home visit – somewhat unheard of these days! It had spread in typical domino fashion; first Oli, Ben and Cassia, then Lydia who predictably caught it having popped back to check on them, and finally myself. I can only describe the effect of full-blown flu as feeling like you've been steamrollered and then reversed over for good measure. Thankfully we are all on the mend and no doubt a few pounds lighter. The implication for Fabian is, of course, that no-one has been able to stay with him for most of the week which has been quite a blow for the poor chap. A few friends have paid him some brief visits, but nothing is quite like having Mum 24/7 as she has done these past 7 months. Annoyingly, we are unable to skype him on demand due to the hospital WiFi timing out very few minutes so rely on him calling us back from the ward phone. I can report though, that his temperatures appear to have stabilised and they have reduced or ceased most of his antibiotic medication so perhaps a release date is imminent? Ironically, our home would be too infectious for him to come back to! So, looking ahead to a better week, we have a couple of family events to celebrate; our wedding anniversary and Oli's 18th. Fabian's homecoming would top that just nicely. Today though, is Mothering Sunday and I would like to honour the total devotion and dedication that Lydia has shown as a mother this past year in the most challenging circumstances.

MARCH 26, 2012

Discharged!

I certainly tempted the Lord's providence by suggesting in my last entry that Fabian might be discharged imminently – and it paid off! Finally after 64 days 8 hours and 12 minutes (but who's counting?) he was given the all clear and sent home armed with a pharmaceutical-sized medicine bag for good measure. To say this is a relief would be an understatement as for the past 3 weeks we have not known what was causing his cycle of temperatures and it was feared this could be a stubborn viral infection. But thankfully, the final culture results confirmed he was clear, though of course he will remain in a vulnerable condition for months to come. There was a nice surprise at the weekend to find Fabian once again appearing in the national press in a feature about children known to the Duchess of Cambridge and traffic to this site went exponential for the day!

So the end of that road and the start of another. Looking ahead, I guess there will be less frequent news to report now that normal family life has resumed (were we ever normal?) but do drop by the site from time to time to check and keep on with your faith for Fabian – thanks for sharing this journey with us until now.

APRIL 22, 2012

Convalescing

OK everyone, time for an update for those of you kind and tenacious enough to keep following our journey. We're now close to 90 days post-transplant and nearing the 100 day marker when any acute conditions effectively become chronic. Wonderfully, there have been little continued signs of GvHD or other side effects as Fabian continues his long convalesence to recovery. He is still on cyclosporin, an immune-suppresant to keep any last vestiges of his own immune system from fighting back though this will gradually be phased out. Trips to the Marsden are frequent and typically take out 2 full days each week although it's always a relief to drive away from daycare after his blood counts have been checked and cleared. We had one worrying occasion when Fabian's legs swelled up inexplicably – a so-called oedema – but after an overnight stay he was sent home with the doctors still scratching their heads wondering what caused this. An expected side-effect of the TBI conditioning has been somnolence (thankfully not flatulence!). This causes sudden onsets of tiredness without warning (I think we parents have been suffering this since first having children).

There are certain practical restrictions on what we can do together with Fabian and this certainly precludes any foreign travel or attending large public events. Keeping the house clean and hygienic with teenagers around is perhaps the biggest challenge and I must confess to recently finding evidence of mice in residence so erm, I hope none of his care team are reading this. Cassia and I completed our first walk for charity yesterday, joining Ian Botham and a host of celebrities raising money for leukaemia and lymphoma research. Sadly, an old college friend mine recently learnt he has lymphoplasmacytic lymphoma so having these personal connections made taking part even more rewarding.

Journeys' end?

I see from the site stats that there continues to be a steady stream of visitors despite no new entries for quite a while. Today though marks a particular milestone in Fabian's journey – the removal of his Hickman line (intravenous catheter). This vital line has served him well for 387 days providing pain-free, easy access for all his medication, blood samples and even nutrition but somewhat inhibited life for a boisterous 10-year-old! The removal procedure was quite straightforward and hopefully, for the last time, he underwent the normal general anaesthetic, joking with the medical team even as his eyelids drooped and then closed. What this also signals is the doctors' confidence in his post-transplant recovery and indeed his recent lumbar puncture confirmed that there were no blast (leukaemic) cells present so we can conservatively say that the transplant has been a total success in eradicating the disease (cue loud Amen!). His hair has certainly grown back with a vengeance (actually, it's a wig..).

Medication and monitoring will of course continue and we trust the residual side effects of his treatment will be minimal. Our biggest concern going forward is Fabian's educational development as he has effectively missed around 40% of schooling since reaching compulsory school age. For him, it is really a question of regaining confidence amongst his peers so perhaps a staged return to school from next term will build this. His school have been very supportive throughout the whole process. Other than that, he has remained predominately healthy and well and giving our rabbits and chickens regular exercise chasing them round the garden. Having avidly watched the Olympics, Fabian has now decided to become a boxer. Now that would be testament to someone who could barely climb out of bed a few months ago!

In closing this blog, it's been a pleasure and a privilege to share our journey with you and hopefully an inspiration to those who may face their own dark times ahead. Thanks too for the great support along the way which has been so pivotal in helping us keep our faith4fabian.

God bless y'all

Darrell (Fabian's sentimental dad)

MARCH 9, 2013

A new chapter
I had thought that my last post was to have been my LAST post. Sadly not.
Since that time, Fabian had been enjoying a near normal life, free of infection and being well in himself. Regular School attendance was not yet possible though he had settled into a routine of home education supplemented by some wonderful tutors. On January 28th we celebrated the anniversary of his transplant which was highlighted by having a double page spread in Hello magazine who had been keen to do a follow up to Fabian's 'royal encounter' story. The year milestone gave us all a psychological lift as by now it was evident that the transplant had totally engrafted and he had passed the high risk point of relapse.
But the cruel nature of this disease was to prove otherwise. Around this time Fabian started feeling pains in his back and stomach and began to lose both his

energy and appetite. His blood counts seemed fine, albeit with some signs of infection, but the medics appeared none too worried. The symptoms, however, worsened and he began to have excruciating abdomen pains for which proprietary painkillers were ineffective. We bravely went ahead with a home party on his 11th birthday, March 2nd and he enjoyed the company of friends and making lego sets. But by evening, Lydia was packed and ready to take him into Kingston Hospital where he was able to receive stronger painkillers. This was followed on Monday by an MRI and ultrasound scan – something that doctors should have undertaken much earlier, for it immediately determined the cause of pain was due to extensive enlargement of his lymph nodes. Yet once again, blood tests revealed no sign of blast cells so we were still optimistic that this was purely a viral infection such as EBV. Kingston transferred us to the Marsden the next day and we found ourselves back in all too familiar surroundings, a place full of emotional memories for us.

It was decided to carry out a bone marrow aspirate as this would confirm or otherwise the root cause of the lymph swelling. I signed the standard consent form for the operation, one that Fabian had endured so many times before. Lydia remained living in while I was back at work and we awaited the outcome.

The waiting was short-lived. Our consultant met us yesterday to confirm in a resigned but matter of fact manner, that the bone marrow contained a high proportion of leukaemic cells. Fabian had been, in his words, 'very unlucky'. I can't say this scenario had not already been played in my head a hundred times but in truth, the reality of hearing it was like a hammer blow. It wasn't unlucky; it was unfair. Massively.

So a new chapter begins with faith4fabian. As to our medical options I shall keep that for a later post. There is but one option – total healing in Jesus Name and Lydia and I would love to know at this time that many of you faithful followers of this blog will join in our prayer for this. "For he shall not die but live and proclaim what The Lord has done" Ps 118:17

This time it's serious

"For we know in part, then we shall know fully" (1 Cor 13:12). These words of St Paul seem to capture our own state of mind concerning the return of Fabian's leukaemia. We know that initially chemo and now a bone marrow transplant have failed to eradicate this aggressive disease, and this in spite of his event-free and sustained health after both first and second remission. So we face this once more and to quote a line, 'this time it's serious'. Our consultants are of the opinion that Fabian deserves, and has every hope of a cure, via a second stem cell transplant (SCT). This is a wonderful lifeline for which we thank God. All the more so as we know we have our reserve sibling donor, Oleander, ready and waiting to offer Fabian this gift. This is the strategy but much needs to be finalised beforehand and an unrelated 10/10 matched donor is also an option if that would provide a better combination of engraftment, GvHD and GvL. Fabian will first undergo an intense block of chemo to get him into remission – a prerequisite for SCT – and this begins on Monday. He has spent the last 2 weeks grumpily complaining about the hospital, the food, us and anyone that dares approach! This is so understandable as we gradually explain to him what he must go through. Fabian has tremendous perception and emotional insight for one so young, often bringing us to tears with his heartfelt remarks; 'Mummy, my body is broken isn't it?', 'Without Oli here it's like a piece of my heart is missing' and 'If I don't feel any pain why can't I go home?". He is equally stoic and this quality will serve him well during the difficult days

ahead as we have been warned that the risk of complication or infection is much higher, often proving more dangerous than the disease itself. Meanwhile, we have been offered a brief period of respite as Fabian has been allowed home for the weekend to recharge his spirit ready for the prolonged stay in hospital. He has always been asking to stay in the Legoland Hotel so that is what we are going to do! Fortuitously, Oli comes home from Uni today so we shall all be together to enjoy the moment. It will be precious.

MARCH 23, 2013

Exciting developments

Sitting in the Marsden next to Fabian whilst he sleeps soundly, a beneficial side effect of the intense chemo block he has just finished. Unfortunately, there are other less pleasant ones such as diarrhoea, sore eyes and loss of appetite which all blight him at present. The strength of the chemo reduced his blood counts to zero within a few days and it will take 2-3 weeks for this to recover sufficiently to be discharged. We expect, though he'll need a second block to achieve remission and in anticipation of this the doctors have applied for funding to use a newer drug, chlorfarabine, that is not yet available on standard protocols. There is a hefty price tag for each cycle so we have to be hopeful that our local PCT is not one where the postcode lottery for funding works against us. Looking ahead to the transplant, we have also heard that Fabian may be offered the chance to join a new clinical trial which will test ground-breaking gene therapy techniques to improve the effectiveness post-transplant of the donor T-cell lymphocytes. In simple terms, this should make them better hunter-killers of leukaemic cells. This may mean a move to Great Ormond Street hospital if all goes ahead. So these are exciting developments for us in terms of accessing the best and latest treatment. Casting back a week, our trip to Legoland was a much-needed oasis for the family – literally, as it was very wet! We followed this on our return with an impromptu birthday party for Fabian, complete with Lego cake that had been kindly donated to us. Easter, though, will be spent on the ward so the traditional egg hunt will be confined to bed 3; but on the bright side, at least we get to avoid this "spring" weather

APRIL 2, 2013

War of attrition

We've now settled into the familiar routine post chemo of daily temperature spikes, antibiotics and waiting for count recovery. It is a war of attrition. The lagged effect of the intensity of this block hit Fabian about 6 days after its completion in the form of neurological symptoms. His personality seemed to have been totally suppressed and for a while he responded to nothing and no-one. Concerned there may be a neural infection the doctors did an MRI and lumbar puncture but thankfully both confirmed this wasn't the case. As anticipated, he has needed a nasal gastric tube inserted since weight loss has become a growing concern. This is something Fabian absolutely detests but it was able to done under general anaesthetic for the LP. Now, in the last 48 hours he is returning to normality and it is a small but joyous thing just to see him take a few bites of food. Despite having a battery of chocolate eggs, this was the first Easter we have seen where our son has not devoured them in quick time! With regards to the potential treatments, we have since heard that funding has been approved for the chlorfarabine and a referral has been made for the immunotherapy trial though both of these will depend on the outcome of his next bone marrow aspirate in 2 weeks time. The extent and depth of research into treatment for leukaemia is phenomenal, often made possible by charitable donation alone as there is insufficient 'return on investment' for the drug giants to prioritise this. Drugs alone, though, will never cure a spiritual cause and we are seeking to understand what roots might have caused this disease so that these can be cut off once and for all.

APRIL 16, 2013

Recovering

Well, we are now into Day 44 of this incarceration, though I myself am not incarcerated – just in-car-seated since my weekly mileage has multiplied. Our wonderful Fabian is finally recovering his blood count (WBC 1.1) and up and about continuing that interminable road to recovery since the chemo block. He is now minus his hair and a few kilos in weight but nothing that won't return in time (although his Kojak pate is nearly matched by brother Ben who actually chooses that style) Mum Lydia has been unstinting at the hospital during this time with occasional overnight relief provided by Oleander whilst she was back from Uni. The relentless march of infections seems to have been stemmed; the worst, a candida fungal infection, led to doctors having to remove his Hickman line. This in itself necessitated transferring to St George's for a couple of days. The frequent monitoring of Fabian's organ and body functions is by now all too familiar; a legacy of the fact that each chemo drug causes unwanted side effects which manifest in every child to a greater or lesser extent. At this stage, after 6 and a half years on and off treatment, the cumulative impact could have been chronic problems but our brave fighter has shown such resilience in mind I'm sure his body will continue to follow suit. We're now awaiting the next bone marrow aspirate which will indicate whether we have achieved remission, but notwithstanding this, a second block of consolidation chemo is a near certainty, this time using super drug chlorfarabine (yay). In between this, Fabian may be given home leave which will be a huge boost for him, not least because I have redecorated his room to look like the hospital ward (, sorry, joke, it's late at night). Meanwhile, it's always a pleasure having friends to visit and we appreciate the effort that that requires – especially trying to get into the place once they arrive! We had another celebrity visitor drop in, Peter Andre, but Fabian wasn't up for the photo opportunity (Mr Andre's loss). The Marsden is a unique environment where an improbable mix of parents, patients and professionals form a tight-knit community, all focused on the single goal of getting discharged from the place. Global issues and threats of nuclear war are strangely distant and actually not very important whilst you are inside. Do keep us in your prayers amongst the many demands in your life, we hope as many as want will be a part of Fabian's healing (James 5:15).

Green shoots

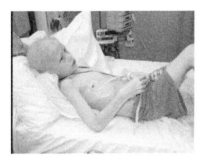

Sibling match

Royal visit

A royal surprise

Homeward bound

Thankful this Christmas

Days of zero

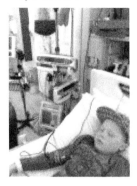

Journey's end

Exciting developments

Preparing for
admission

Summer days

When negative is positive

Setbacks

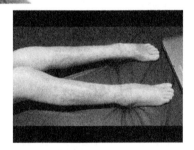

T Cells R Us

T Cells 30 – Leukaemia luv

Times and seasons

Thumbs up

Tanks and thanks

Down but not out

This sucks

Infections,
decisions and
our big G

The longest night

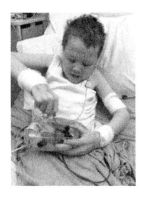

Eleven eleven

APRIL 26, 2013

Onwards and upwards

Much to report since last. Fabian's improving blood count following chemo resulted in him being allowed home late last Friday. Seven weeks hospital stay had certainly fuelled his eagerness to be back in his own room and thankfully, he approved of my redecoration. The weather picked the right time to improve and he was able to enjoy sunshine in the garden and heckling the chickens. Now as we have learnt, being discharged is actually a euphemism for 'see you in daycare tomorrow'. This is usually because a whole host of medication continues and needs to be administered at hospital. So he was indeed back on Monday for prophylaxis drugs and blood tests; routine but time-consuming none the less. The next day though, he and sister Cassia enjoyed a special treat to have been invited to tour the film studios at Elstree. Here, they also met the special effects team who had arranged to create a mould of Fabian's head and hands and produce these in rubber. Not sure what their use will be, but memorable none the less.

The following day proved to be both unpredictable and bizarre. It began with Fabian and I back in daycare whilst Lydia was at another hospital with Ben who needed urgent treatment for a knee injury. Fabian's platelets were extremely low and he needed a transfusion but there wasn't time as we had a not-to-be-missed appointment at Great Ormond Street Hospital to discuss the transplant trial that he is being considered for. The trip there and back took far longer than anticipated and it was early evening by the time we go back to the Marsden where he could finally have the transfusion and this made for a 12 hour day by the time we were all home. Shortly after though, we noticed heavy bleeding around his intravenous line. This wasn't clotting due to his lack of platelets and was going to need more than an elastoplast. So, with blood-soaked Fabian, it was back in the car, this time to Kingston, our shared care hospital where he needed yet another transfusion and an overnight stay. Overall, an exhausting tour of 3 hospitals in one day. We were hugely relieved to learn that the result of last week's bone marrow aspirate confirmed no leukaemic cells present. This makes all the heavy chemo feel worth it – and I don't mean L'Oreal! Thankfully then his disease can still be controlled by drugs alone but as has been evident, this is not a satisfactory solution. The new immunotherapy treatment now available is now our preferred option. We were excited to find out more about this trial and to learn it is truly at the cutting edge of blood cancer treatment internationally with only a handful of patients receiving this treatment to date. Early findings from the States are favourable, even making headline news with its results. Side effects from GvHD are greatly minimised although the overall impact of toxicity is still unclear. What feels so right about this new approach is that it essentially uses the power of the body's own immune system – with a little T cell modification – to heal itself rather than using a drugs-based approach. And coupled with the potential benefit to improving treatments for future children, joining this research trial seems absolutely right. Our donor is yet to be confirmed but we will need to transfer to GOSH with a transplant date planned for early to mid-June. Many visits needed before then and we will certainly get to know the route to WC1 intimately (if not the lack of parking!). Still in his 'week off', Fabian is back in hospital, this time with an infection. He has become well-known on the oncology circuit and always gets a warm welcome from the medical staff, though always apologising for seeing him back again. This is a tiring journey which we could not complete without our Heavenly Father who gives strength to the weary. Onwards and upwards.

Prayer and preparation

To those of who that pray for Fabian – and I know many do – I want to encourage you that your prayers offered in faith most certainly make a difference. Seeing him now, in remission and in such good health following the hammering chemo he received only weeks ago is testament to this. In fact until recently our consultant described him as 'very frail' yet he has bounced back beyond medical expectation. Yes, he had an infection which meant an unscheduled 5 day hospital stay and his neutrophil count remains low but his overall recovery has been rapid given the parlous state of his bone marrow. This augers well for preparing him for transplant as he will need to be in the best physical condition going into this most dangerous procedure. For that reason, the treatment plan is to keep Fabian on low level (maintenance) chemo for the time being rather than the high dose chlorfarabine that was originally planned. We need wisdom in this decision as the danger of relapse is ever present and would jeopardise the transplant route if that happened. Meanwhile, we know that 13-year-old Cassia will once again be his donor from the point of view that introducing a different donor's stem cells this time around could generate a graft vs. graft reaction as there would be in effect 3 different immune systems all vying for supremacy. The gene therapy approach requires her to give a sizeable sample of blood beforehand that gets couriered to a lab in France, Nantes to be precise, where the T cells are genetically treated with a retrovirus for a 100 days and then returned ready for infusing into Fabian. This may be cutting edge research but actually seems like rather a crude process. The thought of this life-giving sample being lost in freight is unimaginable! I fancy a trip to collect it myself. So we are hoping for an event-free May in preparation for the summer of discontent (as it were). It is also exam season and both Ben and Oli face their own trials in this respect. With all they have witnessed, I'm sure they will do well in Biology. Keep on keeping on.

MAY 14, 2013

Fire with fire

I've titled this entry after the name of this moving video which charts the story of a little girl in the States who underwent similar gene therapy to that which Fabian will receive and had an amazing outcome. It may seem over-dramatised, but the outcomes are true none the less. We really feel honoured to be selected for this ground-breaking trial here in the UK. It's timely for me to share this, as most of today was spent at Great Ormond Street Hospital during which they collected the vital blood sample from Cassia that will be genetically treated ready for infusion into Fabian later in July. To see those test tubes with their precious contents being packaged up was both profound and yet mundane. The bureaucratic paperwork that followed was most certainly mundane but then there are a vast array of researchers and agencies whom we must consent to providing Fabian's treatment data.

I'm also pleased to report that his blood count has bounced back remarkably well. Platelets and neutrophils have tripled in the past week – signs of his marrow getting back into full production. But now maintenance chemo has started up so we expect these will drop again. Nevertheless, we have 3 or 4 weeks before his planned admission so hopefully some nice day trips in between Marsden day-care trips to enjoy. Other signs of new life at home are that our rabbits have produced a clutch of babies and mother hen is sitting on a dozen eggs so the household is feeling quite broody. And on that note, I should end.

MAY 31, 2013

Maintaining remission

Staying in remission is a full-time job. And a very important one. As the days countdown to T-Day we know this aggressive disease could return at any time and jeopardise the outcome of Fabian's planned transplant. Since achieving remission (but not disease free as determined by the MRD test) he has been on maintenance therapy as an outpatient and struggling to recover his blood counts which frustratingly seesaw like a rollercoaster. His bone marrow remains desperately frail having been transplanted once and then hammered by the strongest dose of chemo permissible. But we were heartened by the latest MRD result which showed a 10-fold reduction in leukaemic cells from last time to a staggeringly low 2 cells per 100,000. And yet even at that level, left untreated the leukaemia would ultimately come back whether in weeks, months or years. They call this scenario the sword of Damocles. Readers may like to google for the full story!

So Fabian is trying to enjoy these days at home in between hospital trips and generally keeping well. He had a lovely day at the zoo and has been racing up and down on his new go-kart, a generous gift from the Shooting Star trust. Our chicks hatched against all odds and together with the baby bunnies (minus one deceased) they are a reminder to us of the wonder and fragility of new life. Your continued prayer is valued and Fabian knows he is in the hearts of many.

Preparing for admission

Ok, so no news is good news, right? Indeed, no major developments to report as we count down the days to admission. Fabian assiduously marks his calendar each day as that time approaches, but it is hardly what any 11-year-old boy would look forward to; weeks of confinement in probable isolation during what might even be a decent summer. He is a very reluctant transplant patient, stating with certainty that he does not require one now that he feels better. And we all wish that were true. He well remembers his first transplant in January 2012 and asks whether he will get sick and lose weight again – we hope not. At least he will be going in plumped up after the steroid effect boosted his appetite these last few weeks and he has been overdosing on cheese strings and pasta.

Now that we have transferred to Great Ormond Street for the procedure we have had to be inducted into the GOSH way of doing things. This is altogether more strict than the Marsden in terms of what is, and is not permissible on the ward. The risk of infection is the biggest concern and all manner of protocols are put in place to limit this. Not so long ago the children were kept in 'plastic bubbles' so I'm glad things have moved on from that! Visiting is heavily restricted and limited to viewing through a window only so Skype is likely to become the communication tool of choice. Everyone is expecting that engraftment will be straightforward and quick, since Cassia of course is the same donor. She has had to undergo her own medical and psychological assessment during which her only concern was the possibility of waking up in the middle of sedation! She is very brave to do this all again and joins a very elite group of sibling double donors.

We've managed a few memorable events for Fabian; holding a BBQ for his choice of guests and a special meal for the family at Jamie Oliver's Fifteen restaurant, driven there by stretch limo. We all enjoyed being photographed by tourists who assumed we were celebs, but to us of course, Fabian is. Everyone is rooting for him as we go into this final phase of treatment and your prayers and best wishes for him mean everything.

JUNE 25, 2013

T day

I'm here with Fabian on the eve of T-day, his transplant. It's been a week since his admission and the unwelcome side effect of the pre-conditioning chemo has been to cause him the usual loss of appetite coupled with frequent bouts of diarrhoea and vomiting. Thankfully, he consented to having an NG tube inserted which will at least mean he gets the nutrition he needs. The unfamiliar staff and environment here at GOSH is taking Fabian some getting used to, but having Lydia with him provides him constant reassurance that all will be fine. Isolation is, of course, a tedious pain but a necessary one. At least there are 2 weeks of Wimbledon coverage ahead. Cassia is here too, going through prelims ready for her big day tomorrow. She will spend the night in an adjacent ward as it's an early start for the stem cell harvesting procedure. The transplant itself will take places a few hours later and as before, will seem like an anti-climax after all the buildup. Then all we can do is wait for the all-important white blood count to rise, signifying engraftment. The REALLY important stage comes later in August when the modified T cells will be infused. I guess that will be another T day.
Our encouragement remains in the Lord. Psalm 147:3 "He renews our hopes and heals our bodies"

Post transplant and unexpected post

Well, we are the right side of transplant - no longer 'pre' but 'post'. However, what ought to have been a straightforward harvesting procedure for Cassia turned into something far more protracted as surgeons were unable to collect the required WB cells per ml and ended up having to take a far larger blood quantity than planned. This has left her feeling somewhat worse for wear and extremely fatigued after such a large loss of blood and two, rather one puncture wounds. She has been truly brave undergoing this procedure again and is having well-deserved r+r at home. The net result is that engraftment is now likely to take longer given the lower percentage of stem cells so inevitably this means longer isolation and continued risk of infection for Fabian (groan). At T+4 he is suffering the side effects of mucositis and constant pain for which he has morphine. A neat little hand-held controller rather like a TV remote allows him to regulate the dose as required. There are never less than 3 intravenous lines into him at any one-time supplying nutrition, antibiotics and fluids. This makes manoeuvring round his cramped room even less practical. The NG feeding tube was duly thrown up and he is canny enough to charge us £10 to have it reinserted! All for the good cause of buying a remote-control tank one day.

We had an unexpected letter postmarked St James Palace. It was from the Duke of Cambridge who wanted to wish Fabian well. I am impressed that William and Kate obviously follow his progress as they keep abreast of his current treatment and status. I'm sure they will make wonderful parents with all the consideration they show for children. Fabian says hi to all his global followers which now span every continent (see visitor map). Keep willing him on and for the new stem cells to start producing white cells. With British tennis players

doing unusually well at Wimbledon, I'm feeling
positive!

Summer days

Watching warm summer days pass by from the confines
of his room is no fun for Fabian. It's tough to seem to
see him on my visits feeling down and not being able to
fix that – my attempts at humour are not even funny.
He is the bravest boy to endure this but the continuing
hospitalisation inevitably takes its toll on his wellbeing.
We did enjoy watching the Wimbledon final together,
good object lesson in winning against adversity.
With each passing day we await signs of engraftment,
which at D+14 could be imminent. Thankfully, he has
stayed infection free with the occasional temperature
spikes that are immediately dampened with a barrage of
antibiotics. Eating and drinking is still something to
hope for, so all his nutrition and fluids needs continue
to be given intravenously. Last weekend we had the use
of one of the hospital's flats so managed some family
time together in the heart of WC1 – one of the perks of
having a long-term in patient! We also heard the sad
news that a contemporary of Fabian's at the Marsden,
and someone who met the Royals with him in 2011, lost
his long battle with acute myeloid leukaemia. He is, for
sure, in a better pain-free place, but a tragic loss
nonetheless.

Grow cells grow!

Five weeks post-transplant and I guess many of you are wondering about engraftment. Well so am I, hence the silence hitherto. I can, though, now report that Fabian's blood count hit the all-important 2.0 WBC level but promptly dropped back once they reduced his GCSF dose which is given to artificially boost the WBC. Remember the chant – 'Grow cells grow'. No-one on staff is particularly worried as he has been doing really well clinically and they are not counting the days, as we do. One sure sign that the new stem cells are engrafting is the recent onset of GvHD which in Fabian's case means he has a nasty all-over itchy skin rash. He looks a sorry sight in the buff but there is a lot in the medical armoury to relieve the discomfort, mainly steroid creams and we are hoping the rash will dissipate in due course. Today was bone marrow aspirate day and we'll know by Friday whether his MRD has remained negligible meaning no further development of leukaemia since the last round of chemo. Please pray for an MRD negative reading! Life in room 6 continues into the 7th week for Lydia and Fabian. I am surprised they have not been etching the days into the wall, as prisoners do. Other families have come and gone, not all with positive outcomes sadly. The parent's room is a place where hopes and fears are shared and one cannot help feeling a twinge of guilt if ones' own child is doing better than another. The isolation restrictions are continuing but are somewhat 'relaxed' at the weekend when a certain Sister is not on duty! For example, visitors can sneak onto the ward and view loved ones through the glass and talk to them via intercom. Cassia did this and she and Fabian placed their hands together through the glass à la Kirk-Spock movie style. We're hoping for a release date in the next couple of weeks subject to many variables most of which we cannot predict or control. And that reminds me about Jesus' words not to worry about tomorrow (Matt 6:34).

AUGUST 8, 2013

When negative is positive

In most of life's situations, a negative result is generally bad. Not so for an MRD test. We've had Fabian's result back and he is MRD negative which confirms there is now no detectable trace of leukaemia in his marrow – a clear answer to my prayer request last entry. This MRD is also a better result than the one 2 months ago, indicating that the disease has continued to respond to chemo and the transplant. This is more of a relief than a surprise and it keeps us on track for the T-cell infusion at the end of the month – the real cure. The two other children presently in the trial have sadly had their transplants fail and can therefore no longer continue with it so I guess all researchers' eyes will now be on 'fighting Fabian'. Confirmation also that he has fully engrafted and maintained the minimum neutrophil count long enough for doctors to downgrade his isolation restrictions from red to yellow (think DefCon rating). This was great news for Fabian who was immediately on the phone to tell us excitedly that he's going to be free. Once they disconnected his meds he was out the room like a shot and into the corridor, accosting hapless passers by with tales of his captivity. It's good to see him so cheered up, even more so the next day when Ben and Cassia visited and were able to hug their brother for the first time in over 6 weeks (Cassia took a dozen snaps to record the occasion!). All that remains is for him to be self-sustaining in food and fluids and to this end we are likely to agree for a 'PEG' to be inserted in his stomach. This is rather like a valve through which he can be fed and is an alternative to the naso-gastric tube which he so hates. The GvHD has also receded though he'll remain on steroids for a while to combat the continuing temps.

On a less sanguine note, I well remember the same scenario 18 months ago following the first transplant when hopes were high. We are not kidding ourselves that we are out of the woods by any means but we do rejoice with you who also rejoice for each step he makes towards being cancer-free.

AUGUST 25, 2013

Bad temperature stops play

It's been a frustrating couple of weeks since I last wrote. The end has been in sight for days now but doctors have been reluctant to give the green light for Fabian's discharge, so we remain on amber. He has stayed remarkably well during this time, with blood counts steadily rising and no infections or post-transplant complications. Well not exactly. Today he had been given special dispensation to go home for the day to join his grandad for his 80th birthday celebration. This was to be quite a family occasion and something he had been looking forward to, even if it meant coming back into hospital. Then the first obs this morning showed a temperature over 39C so the doctor's rule applied – feeling rather like the untimely bad light stopping play decision of the umpires in the 5th test – that he could not go. A horrible blow which did nothing to lift his spirits. Still, by the wonders of Skype he was able to 'join' the celebrations nonetheless. So now we must await the result of blood cultures to determine the cause, whether bacterial or viral but I suspect it will subside in a day or so as has often been the case in the past. Spiking temperatures are normal routine following a BMT but one cannot be too careful.

So we approach the end of the 10th week here at GOSH and it has been a slog. The delay in Fabian engrafting has also put back the T cell infusion which is now scheduled for mid-September but this has no bearing on the outcome of the trial. Despite adversity, we continue to thank God for his wellbeing.

SEPTEMBER 1, 2013

Setbacks

Days become weeks and weeks become months. Here we still are, another week on with no firm discharge date in place. In fact, following his spiked temperature last Sunday, Fabian took a turn for the worse as our old friend GvHD returned with its accompanying disruption to normal bodily functions. The skin rash, which is symptomatic of this post-transplant reaction, is rather unpleasant so I thought I'd include a photo with this entry to illustrate the point! So back on steroids, immune-suppressants, GCSF etc. All clinical reasons to keep him in hospital. However, I can report that there have been signs of improvement and at least a treat for Fabian has been the doctor's decision to allow him brief periods outside. Armed with his scooter, he has loved these brief forays into the nearby park, even though he catches attention with his bald head and mask. The temptation to jump on a bus and head for home is strong! But soon enough it's medication time and back to Fox ward he goes. I'll say a word about the nursing staff, since the press is currently projecting the NHS as full of disgruntled nurses, most of whom would leave given the chance. Our observation is otherwise and we find them always professional and committed. Each nurse relates very differently to Fabian but they all enjoy being his carer when their turn comes round.

In terms of the genetic treatment we have had a setback in that the lab have been unable to generate enough T cells from the original sample and now require Cassia to give further blood. This will delay the infusion into Fabian by a further 6 weeks 😖 though we are assured by our consultant this will have no bearing on the overall outcome (bear in mind hardly anyone else has had this treatment!). I'm praying for more patience, but please God, hurry up.

SEPTEMBER 14, 2013

Home; but not alone

I can't believe I've waited nearly a week to report that Fabian was actually discharged! Perhaps it was because I half expected him to be re-admitted within a day or so, but nevertheless he and Lydia are back after 81 days on Fox ward and another chapter in our seven-year journey of treatment ends. Of course, they weren't going to let him go without an accompanying shed load of medication and paraphernalia, all of which has turned our kitchen into a nurse's station. Preparing and administering these drugs together with taking obs and fluids through his PEG takes upwards of a couple of hours a day but it is certainly more preferable being at home with family than in the isolation unit. Community nurses come to the house weekly to take bloods and he'll need to attend daycare clinic regularly at GOSH so it's not like we are going to miss them! The meds will gradually reduce as his immunity strengthens and I'm pleased to say his most recent bone marrow check returned another negative result; so still in total remission, praise God.

One of Fabian's first priorities was to purchase the remote-controlled tank he had been saving for. He is so pleased to be home, just to be free to mess around not being connected up to a machine or being prodded and poked by medical staff every few hours. He was so observant, noticing every minor change in the house since he had been away. It made me realise how such small things had become significant for him having been away so long.

Fabian's return also coincided with the start of a new school year and I can muse on the fact I now have a child in each sector of the education system; higher, further, secondary and primary. Fabian obviously isn't able to return just yet and will resume his home education for the time being but its packed lunches and school runs for the others. Somehow it's starting to feel more normal again.

OCTOBER 22, 2013

Steady growth

Yes, it's been a while. But be assured if there were developments to report – both good and bad – faith4fabian readers would be the first to hear. So there haven't been. And that of course is a good development in that Fabian has been doing just fine since his homecoming just over 5 weeks ago. Cell by cell his immunity is rebuilding itself and the all-important white cell count is rising. It's not all plain sailing and his blood count tracker over time resembles the FTSE 100, steady growth over time but many highs and lows. This means regular transfusions, particularly of platelets, the all-important anti-clotting agent. He is actually allergic to them and nonchalantly reminds the nurses of this on each occasion as if they should all know by now (a simple anti-histamine dose overcomes the allergy). There's also been the odd infection or raised CRP marker (irregular kidney function) which have meant a couple of stays at our local hospital. but this is all small fry compared to what many others experience post-transplant and as ever we are grateful to God for His continuing grace for Fabian. The date for the T cell infusion has drifted back to early November but there are no concerns, only impatience! We are one of a handful of families being filmed as part of a documentary following the development and progress of the new immunotherapy treatment. It'll remain under wraps until there are some actual results to shout about and naturally we want Fabian to be one of the first successful recipients of the treatment in which case I'll be pushing for a red carpet premiere of the film in Leicester Square. Elsewhere, family life presents us with many challenges, some unforeseen, many unwanted, all of our lives having been impacted by this journey we share with Fabian. We couldn't do it alone and neither were we meant to.

NOVEMBER 9, 2013

Preparing for T Day

So I'm writing this entry from an all too familiar setting; Fox ward at Great Ormond Street. Yes, we're back here for the final treatment phase, somewhat overdue but timely nonetheless. Fabian's most recent bone marrow aspirate indicated a very small but measurable amount of residual disease. Despite this unwelcome news, he is otherwise in a very good state to receive the modified T cells next week. For example, Fabian has sufficient EBV, a naturally occurring virus, with which to 'trigger' the T cells into attack mode -an absolute pre-requisite for them to take on the leukaemia cells too and ensure they remain long term in his immune system. It's clear the bone marrow transplants haven't been totally effective in eradicating this disease so we are left with all hope resting on the modified cells to do the job once and for all.

Before that, Fabian has to undergo a short chemo protocol to 'dampen' his immunity in readiness for the T cells. We're not expecting any side effects from this dose and we know the routine well by now. Do pray that he tolerates the chemo.

The film crew has been ever present recently, capturing random activities at home and in hospital for the forthcoming documentary. We've been lent a video camera with which to record events when they're not around – I call it the Fabcam. Not that there's much to film whilst stuck on the ward whiling away the time. I'll update again post T day.

NOVEMBER 16, 2013

T Cells R Us

It's official. Fabian is now the recipient of genetically-modified T cells (lymphocytes) in this cutting-edge clinical trial that we believe will cure him of leukaemia. But what an anti-climax! On T Day itself he first underwent a standard bone marrow aspirate to determine his pre-treatment level (we still await results). Then the cells arrived amid a flurry of activity with nurses and doctors all checking and double-checking that Fabian was indeed Fabian and they that they had in fact got the right test tubes. Just prior to this, our consultant, a rather eminent professor of haemotology, had given Fabian a final check over and pronounced him 'looking better than I have ever seen him'. He then wished us luck and I thanked him, unable to hold back a brief upsurge of emotion in my gratitude for his ground-breaking work. There was just 5ml of modified cells – 52 million of them to be precise. How could that seemingly small amount of innocuous fluid be a life-saver for our son? They had actually hoped to generate more but Cassia's original blood donation had not produced sufficient T cells. This ought not to matter as once inside Fabian they will multiply rapidly. The infusion itself was a few short minutes, all captured on film by the ITV crew who were clearly not going to miss the moment. Fabian is a reluctant star, unaware of his starring role in being one of the first children to undergo immunotherapy. You will no doubt enjoy his understated performance when the film is finally aired. After it was over we were given the empty vials as mementos and calmed down with a cup of tea (the ultimate medication). Fabian though was subject to round the clock observation in case of unexpected side effects. The similar trial in the U.S. had caused a number of patients to require ICU following their infused cells but much has been learnt from that experience. Nevertheless, doctors were cautious but yet there was no adverse reaction and just 24 hours later Lydia was able to take him outside to play on the swings! He continues to do well and should be discharged early next week. Monthly BMAs will be used to determine the return or not of the disease so we will have a rather nervous wait for results each time. Cancer sufferers will recognise this wait and see existence as the so-called 'sword of Damocles'. But our hope is in the Lord and in Him we trust (constant note to self). Thanks to all of you for standing with us!

NOVEMBER 20, 2013

'One shall rout a thousand'

Check this out – our consultant has told us an awesome statistic; he said one modified T-Cell could destroy a thousand leukaemic cells! This immediately reminded me of that old testament scripture 'one of you shall rout a thousand, because the Lord your God fights for you'

(Josh 23:10). This was spoken by God to Joshua on how he was to possess the promised land and rid it of his enemies and I believe is surely a prophetic statement that speaks to Fabian's cellular-battle within. Promised land equals health and wholeness – enemies equal cancer cells. I'm sure this prompting was an encouragement from God because at the same time the consultant despondently informed us that the latest MRD, taken just pre-treatment has confirmed an increase in disease at the molecular level to one in 10,000, broadly equating to a billion leukaemic cells and growing. So friends, the battle we now know, is very real and pressing. Every one of those precious 52 million fighter cells needs to achieve its potential and destroy AT LEAST a thousand blast cells. Thankfully, the T cells should grow and even out the odds. At the moment it feels like Spartans v Persians.

Now here is my crazy Dad idea... I ask each one of you faithful followers of faith4fabian to sponsor one T cell in prayer to do its job. A cool way to show your support is by 'liking' the dedicated facebook page that I've created for this purpose. If we reach one thousand likes, we rout a million cells – simples! I'd like to aim even higher and with similar page promotions I've seen going viral, anything is possible. When Fabian sees that total rise each day he will be massively encouraged. Ok everyone, start trending...

DECEMBER 14, 2013

"Cautiously optimistic"
Consultants choose their words carefully and they are certainly not prone to outbursts of emotion. So when ours called last night with the results of Fabian's most recent BMA and said he was cautiously optimistic we

knew it was indeed good news. It has been a month since T Day and this BMA result would be the first – and most important – indicator of whether immunotherapy had worked. We knew the T cells had multiplied, thankfully because of the presence of EBV virus, since the original infusion had been so small and may not have been sufficient to overcome the disease which the last test had confirmed was already returning. Furthermore, Fabian is still struggling to maintain his blood counts due to the tenuous bone marrow engraftment. Last weekend he was close to being neutropaenic and anaemic and required both platelet and Hb transfusions plus GCSF to stimulate white blood production. However, the BMA result showed a zero reading against one marker and reduction of half in the other.. This is unequivocal proof that the leukaemia has been significantly reduced and one can assume that extrapolating this forward he will be disease-free within days or weeks! More importantly for the clinical trial, this has been achieved <u>without</u> the use of drugs. Caution, though, tells me to hold fire on a mega-rave celebration just yet.. We were also told that an unintended consequence has been the loss of all remaining EBV so the concern is that those precious T cells will remain in his body, without which Fabian will have no continued protection. We'll know more after clinic this week.

So I guess the words 'joyful Christmas' take on new meaning for us now. It is truly the best present, other than the true reason for the season. With Christmas approaching, Fabian is looking forward to big sister Oleander coming home from Uni tomorrow and his present list reads like the Argos catalogue. Even the likelihood of family squabbles over the holiday period seems inconsequential compared to the value of togetherness.

DECEMBER 31, 2013

2013 and all that

My last entry for 2013 rounds off what can best be described as a year of ups and downs but thankfully ending on an 'up'. Not that I'm superstitious, but Fabian has only relapsed on odd numbered years – 2011 and 2013 – so 2014 bodes well.

A couple of weeks ago I reported that the first aspirate since T Day showed a significant drop in leukaemic levels and that can only be attributed to the effectiveness of the immunotherapy treatment. A single reading, of course, does not constitute a downward trend so the next aspirate reading mid January will give us enough data to plot a line graph which we hope will confirm this. Meanwhile, we have learnt that the all-important EBV virus which had apparently disappeared was found to be present again so more cause for celebration. Fabian himself continues his run of good health and his fragile immune system is starting to strengthen. A further dose of Cassia's stem cells may be required if his blood counts don't pick up over time. Christmas has been somewhat uneventful with the dreadful weather limiting much outdoor activity or trips. Having received a number of gifts on his present hit list, Fabian claimed it was the best Christmas ever. Not sure his siblings agree, now that they are being peppered with foam darts from his new semi-automatic nerf gun! Time then to recharge and all face 2014 together, whatever it plans to throw at us. Bring it on!

JANUARY 11, 2014

T cells 30 : Leukaemia luv

Happy new year to all our faith4fabian followers!

The analogy of a tennis match comes to mind – hence the title - as I report to you the wonderful news that Fabian's second bone marrow aspirate since the T cell infusion showed no increase in MRD, following the significant drop last time. This is perhaps more meaningful than the previous reading as it confirms that immunotherapy alone is destroying and holding back the cancer. In research terms, I guess this is the best outcome the clinical trial team could have hoped for and certainly our talismanic consultant is elated with Fabian's progress. The nervous waiting and wondering between each aspirate result, though, is emotionally exhausting, so upon hearing it, we didn't leap for joy with whoops of delight but simply felt like a huge internal burden had been lifted at least for another month. A relief too, for the other children. Oli is back at Uni now but a great boost for her as she faces some tough biomedical exams. Doctors remain unsure as to the durability of the T cells; a key indicator of this will be continued absence of B cells leading to a low immunoglobulin level, though that can be replaced artificially. Somehow I wished I'd paid more attention to haemotology at school..

So back to my tennis analogy, it feels like this going to be a five setter with leukaemia having taken the first two sets (through relapse) but prayer and treatment now leveling the match and despite all the rain we've had, it hasn't delayed play!

The dogged film crew remain on hand to capture every key moment. Hours spent waiting for an expected call from our consultant are par for the course. Here is Fabian posing with some of their impressive camera equipment.

New hope please

This entry has been a difficult one for me to post. Our fight against leukaemia, analogous to an epic tennis match, has gone to a tiebreak just when we thought we might go a set up. In reality, I'm sorry to report the latest MRD level is not lower, or even the same as the previous two readings but has in fact risen tenfold. We are still talking low molecular levels but nevertheless this is a blow to our rising optimism. It would appear that the precious T cells have simply dispersed and no longer show up in the cell flow cytometry. The reason for this is not yet understood but in part seems to be because of a lack of EBV, the body's naturally-occurring virus that triggers lymphocyte reproduction. It was always one of the known uncertainties going into the trial but at least the evidence proves the modified cells worked wonders whilst they were still present.

This unwelcome turn of events presents yet another clinical decision to make on Fabian's behalf – should we repeat the process? Well, yes and no. To paraphrase Einstein, there is no point repeating the same things and expecting a different result. But the recognition of the importance of EBV means that the next time around the team would infuse the T cells together with an artificial EBV vaccine, hopefully ensuring they persist for longer. This has never been attempted anywhere worldwide. There are, however, several immune-related factors that could inhibit this and rather perversely, we would have to wait for the disease to progress to full relapse before doctors can determine whether these factors would negate repeating the T cells.

As I write, our feeling is to proceed with harvesting more of Cassia's T cells to begin the modification process in the event that they may be needed later on should disease levels rise. This means we'll need to leave the CD19 trial and therefore ongoing treatment cannot be met from the research funds. Furthermore, the hospital ethics committee will need to clear this experimental treatment and Cassia requires hospital approval to donate for a third time. Neither she or Fabian should be used as guinea pigs! We also know that the American version of this treatment has achieved better outcomes and that it could become available, probably in Germany, within a year. There is also the possibility of accessing this in the U.S. but the likelihood of being accepted onto their trial as a non U.S citizen is remote. Not to mention the cost that would run into hundreds of thousands of dollars.

And yet new research on MRD outcomes shows that at least a third of children with the same level of disease as Fabian don't relapse and go on to enjoy a good quality of life for many years. Since he has been such a fighter, Fabian has every chance of being the one in three. The next BMA will tell us more. Meanwhile, we feel more dependent on God than ever to work a miracle. It may come through T cells or divine intervention, we don't mind. New balls and new hope please!

MARCH 6, 2014

A question of ethics

Facing a panel of experts on the hospital ethics committee was tough, but reassuring. We met with them the other day to debate the rights and wrongs of putting Fabian through, yet more, experimental therapy. As parents, we had to argue on his behalf our personal conviction that further treatment is both ethical and justified. We also spoke on behalf of his 3 siblings, whose voice also needed to be heard as they have carried much unspoken pain these last 8 years. Our excellent consultant made a strong clinical case for the new science he is proposing. In fact, Fabian is spearheading a whole new approach in the type of immunotherapy that future leukaemia sufferers will receive. Less than two years ago, none of these options would be available to us, so whilst being hugely grateful for what we have, there is also the sense that in a few years' time, even more advances will have been made that increase curative outcomes. We've yet to receive the panel's recommendation but their initial feedback was that the burden of treatment does not outweigh the benefit and that it would be appropriate to proceed. This gives us great reassurance that we are all doing what is best for Fabian and our family so now we are ready to press on.

Later that day, he was due to have a marrow aspirate to check the level of disease – vital to see what is going on. But it was not to be. Just shortly before going to theatre, he sneakily found a couple of biscuits and munched them down, instantly rendering an anaesthetic too dangerous. Try making a 12-year-old fast all day – not easy! It was also a shame because they had planned to remove his gastrostomic tube which has become a real nuisance. Fabian is concerned that once removed, the resulting hole in his stomach will make him look like he's been shot.. Cassia will donate her blood next week and that will be sent to the lab for modification. At this stage, no-one knows if it will be needed but the process takes two months to complete so needs to get started. On the 2nd March, we celebrated Fabian's 12th birthday. Many of his friends came for the party which began with a trip to watch the Lego movie, a truly rollercoaster film. Back home, we received an unannounced visit from a Korean pastor who had come to pray for Fabian' healing. It was truly moving as children and parents all crowded into the lounge to join together in prayer and God definitely turned up for the party!

Times and seasons

The Book of Ecclesiastes speaks of the different times and seasons in our lives and declares, 'He has made all things beautiful in its time' Ecc 3:11. This is an encouragement, even though events seem far from beautiful right now. At the time of my last entry we had hoped the rising MRD disease level would stabilise, not least because MRD research tells us there was a 28% statistical chance of that happening. The trouble with stats is that that is all they are. So when we learnt that last week's bone marrow aspirate has confirmed a further tenfold rise in leukaemic levels, we're reminded that hope is not measured in percentages. At the same time as that operation, we found Fabian had developed a suspicious lump. Doctors immediately scanned this by ultrasound as it was felt this was due to a localised relapse, even though he has not quite reached 'frank relapse' in his marrow. Since leukaemia is systemic, rather than metastatic, it doesn't matter where the disease shows up, it will end up everywhere. We therefore have to accept this state of affairs and proceed as best we can in continued faith and further treatment. The immediate need is to establish the cause of the lump, so Fabian will have a biopsy performed on it as soon as practicable, together with a lumbar puncture to check the spinal fluid for disease and an intrathecal chemo injection into the CNS for good measure. If the biopsy confirms it is leukaemic, they will use radiotherapy targeted at the area. This could mean daily hospital trips for two weeks. We've also agreed a plan to start him on maintenance level chemotherapy so as to slow the marrow disease growth long enough until the modified T cells are ready. Cassia gave her blood for these last week – indeed more than twice the anticipated amount so that nothing is left to chance in terms of generating sufficient cells. She is truly a saviour sister to donate more life-giving blood to her brother and remains most humble, not seeking any attention because of this for herself. We returned to the Marsden to reacquaint ourselves with our original consultant who will now oversee Fabian's treatment up until the T cells are ready sometime in May. Many memories flooded back. Fabian is an old warhorse to the staff there though it is a strange irony to be greeted with the welcome 'nice to see you back, Fabian'. Returning to my times and seasons theme, I believe this is a time to pray and not give up. The parable of the persistent widow tells us 'that at all times we should pray and not to lose heart' Luke 18:1. We are so grateful for those of you that do. Following the mysterious pastor episode (see previous entry), I also received prayer on behalf of Fabian from Dr Randy Clark, renown for his healing ministry and one- time minister during the Toronto outpouring. God is no respecter of persons – even the dogs eat the crumbs from the table (Matt 7:28). Fabian himself remains sanguine, despite all. He has hopes and dreams to fulfil, so Lego Master Builders, watch out!

APRIL 7, 2014

Something positive

I've been waiting for something positive to post and today we actually received some positive news – that the particular strain of Fabian's leukaemia is still positive. Feeling confused? Well, biomedical devotees of this blog may recall that each leukaemia is identifiable by a protein marker which in Fabian's case is known as CD19 +ve. This information is vital to the efficacy of the immunotherapy as the T cells are engineered to only recognise that marker and the real fear was that following the failure of the first T cell infusion, the disease may have mutated into CD19-ve (cancers have a habit of being remarkably clever when resisting attack).

Thankfully then, this is not the case and this means it is full steam ahead with the new batch of T cells next month (cue loud applause). The recent biopsy though, did sadly confirm the lump was cancerous. The most effective, if horrendous, treatment for this is radiotherapy and this is set to start straight after Easter on a daily basis for two weeks. Because it is localised, Fabian will have to have a lead apron shaped around the area to protect other vital organs. He's also back on a low regimen chemo protocol just to keep disease levels in check. As anticipated, this is knocking his blood counts for six so we're back to our old friend neutropaenia rearing its annoying head.

People always want to know how Fabian is coping and my answer is always to say better than expected. I'm honestly in awe of his mental toughness to keep going despite the seemingly endless hospital trips and treatment and the perpetual inconvenience of having intravenous lines and blood tests. Most of all, I know he is not afraid even when all of us who know and love him are. Please, if you can, pray that the side effects are minimal and that the disease is held at MRD level.

APRIL 30, 2014

Staying positive

It's not every day you have to manage two of your children that have conflicting appointments in different hospitals. Today was however, such a day with Fabian needing his daily radiotherapy at the Marsden whilst Cassia needed to be at St Marys for her own follow-up. It has already been 'one of those weeks' that has comprised long days spent in daycare waiting on drugs, transfusions or consultations. At times, it seems the coordination of our medical world would keep an administrator fully employed. It is tiring. We have to keep the outcome in sight as we attend daily with Fabian for his treatment and I'm pleased to say the radiotherapy is visibly reducing the leukaemic lump. We now have dates for the T cell therapy and our T Day will be later in May. This requires a short stay in Great Ormond Street for a course of chemo and follow up observation. We've been told that the lab in Nantes has generated a decent sized genetically modified sample so it augers well and the vaccine approach this time should make the difference between success and failure. I recently attended a cancer research conference and there is huge optimism around achieving a cure for certain blood cancers within a matter of years. Fabian's therapy is just one of a new breed of personalised medicine therapies that have become possible since the mapping of the human genome and enabled scientists to identify the specific genetic mutations of an individual's cancer. One could argue there has never been a better time to be diagnosed! We're therefore keeping positive for Fabian's outcome, against the clinical odds. His courage and fortitude persist beyond his years, whether it is having a deep intramuscular injection into his thigh or having to lay naked whilst nurses prepare him for radiotherapy; seeing his hair fall out (for the third time) seems par for the course for him. Keep standing with us.

MAY 13, 2014

Thumbs up

Another milestone passed as we completed our brief return for treatment at the Marsden and head back once again to the more illustrious environment at Great Ormond Street. I don't know that we have a preference – each hospital has their pros and cons – but both unequivocally offer a fantastic level of expertise, care and support.

The radiotherapy completed with glowing results (sorry, couldn't resist that) and the tumour caused by relapse appears to have been destroyed. Today, Fabian had a bone marrow aspirate and intrathecal chemotherapy and the result will tell us how his disease has responded to the low level chemo protocol over the last two months. As they administered the anaestheia, he chirpily drifted into unconsciousness, reminding us he was 'off to have a kip'. We used to find this moment quite emotional but the cheer repetitiveness of this procedure has anaesthatised *us* against anxiety. The modified T cells are a little delayed and are not now planned for infusion until early June. We understand the new vaccination approach they will use is now standard procedure on the international trial and this change was confirmed by what was learnt from treating Fabian. We therefore feel that far from being a 'guinea pig', Fabian is in fact a pioneer, in the forefront of immunotherapy treatment. He of course, does not quite see it that way but we and many others are immensely proud that he has stayed the distance and kept his spirits intact. Many of you will have read the recent media attention surrounding Stephen Sutton, another young man fighting life-threatening cancer and the image of him giving a thumbs-up generated a huge fund-raising response across the world. That gesture is a powerful, yet simple symbol of inner strength and one which Fabian has always used himself. So do join us by giving him a big thumbs up wherever you are reading this – and send us a selfie if you dare!

JUNE 2, 2014

Last stop

There are two big events coming up in my diary,
coincidentally both on or around the same day. One is
the start of the World Cup – come on England! (odds
are not looking good though) and the other date, more
importantly, is Fabian's T-Day – come on you chimeric
antigen receptor T cells! (slightly longer odds at around
one million to one). I jest, of course, as the figures are
misleading. Those of you who recall my 'one shall rout
a thousand' analogy last time, know that even a few
million of these killer cells will destroy a billion or more
leukaemic ones. In my last post, I mentioned Fabian
having had another aspirate to check disease level. This
turned out to be 25% lower than the previous reading
(around 6 cells per thousand) so we are thankful he is
still chemo sensitive. It's not quite where we wanted to
be as it represents a high MRD level but we'll take any
positives. He also continues to remain asymptomatic
and in reasonable health although requiring regular
platelet and Hb infusions. His last was 500ml and took
5 hours to infuse! Staring at the drip line for that long
felt worse than watching paint dry. We've now begun
the individually-tailored protocol leading up to T day;
this has meant a number of baseline tests and starting
an intense chemo cocktail designed to deplete his
lymphocyte count to 'make space' for the modified
cells. So it's back to hospital later this week to stay up
to, and for a short while after the big event. It's almost a
year to the day since Fabian's transplant so it will be a
bitter sweet anniversary to be back in isolation on Fox
ward. By way of a send off, parents and pupils at his
school had generously contributed to buy him a top of
the range Lego kit, something that will give hours of
pleasure to our master builder.

We're probably facing the last stop in terms of treatment on this epic journey. There will be no further therapy trials offered if this one fails. One can only remain sanguine when reflecting on this, but the clinical facts can be downright depressing, if truth be told. Yet the biblical example of Job is a huge aspiration to us. On hearing the worst conceivable news, he never blamed God but instead, worshipped Him. Albeit he argued with Him later on and I have to confess to having had a few moans myself, but we do continue to lean on God and the support of others. Will update you all next week

JUNE 11, 2014

Tanks and thanks

Well, after all the hype, our T Day came and went in underwhelming fashion. The build up to this, Fabian's second round of immunotherapy, has seemed hugely drawn out so we did not approach today with the same alacrity as on the previous occasion. It is also sobering to know that this was possibly the last treatment for leukaemia he will ever receive, though not a feeling shared by Fabian who would be elated. The day began with a standard bone marrow aspirate that will provide a baseline level going into the therapy. Fabian's stock phrase just before 'going under' is "see you on the other side" which of course, has a rather different connotation to what he actually means! He recovered well and the cells arrived shortly after lunch accompanied by a small army of nurses and doctors. There was a fear that he might experience a cytokine reaction from the cells and that this would be life-threatening. Since there is no identical precedent to this procedure, one could say the doctors were playing it uber-safe. Vials of hydrocortisone and adrenalin were to hand if a reaction had occurred – the use of which would have rendered the T cells useless and that would be that. Thankfully, this was not the case and within minutes of the infusion Fabian was back to his Lego build from which he had been so rudely interrupted by this procedure, cancer-curing though it may be. There will be a further top up tomorrow and then we wait and see. The EBV virus was administered earlier in the week and it is this that should activate the T cells to multiply and continue to regenerate. To help Fabian understand the process, he's called them his tank cells which he visualises going through his blood blasting the bad cells to bits. Cue battle of Kursk war clips and the analogy is complete, except that unlike those panzers, let's hope *his* tank cells won't run out of gas.

I'll end this entry with another T - thanks. Thanks to our medical team who have given us this unexpected possibility and thank you to God for making possible the unexpected. Here is positive Fabian giving you all the thumbs up!

`

JULY 14, 2014

Down but not out

Regular followers will note I have been offline for the entire duration of the World Cup. This is pure coincidence, I assure you, as had there been news to tell that would have been my first priority (the fact that the tournament was totally absorbing probably distracted me nonetheless).

I know many of you will have been keeping those T for tank cells in your prayers and it has been a constant burden on our minds as we awaited the BMA that would give us the first results. From a symptom point of view,

Fabian has been perfectly fine with no indication of the immune battle taking place within, which ironically was what we wanted to see. For instance, the EBV vaccine that was injected ought to have caused a rash to show the fightback – but there was nothing. No sign either of any 'cytokine storm' that has been the hallmark in the U.S. trials. Just regular trips to our local for platelet and Hb infusions (but by no means minor inconveniences!). But now he has had the BMA together with more vaccine and the result we received was totally deflating – there had been no reduction of leukaemia but in fact a near doubling of the MRD level, though it's still well below frank relapse. The principal consultant is on annual leave so we have yet to unpack the why's and wherefore's of this unexpected outcome but my guess is that it will provide little solace as the headline figure suggests that the treatment has possibly failed because at the same point first time around there had been a measurable disease reduction. This is disappointing for all future beneficiaries too, as a breakthrough in this type of immunotherapy seems still to elude doctors.

We are certainly down but by no means out. Where man's works end, God's begin! In fact, the night following the result, a healing evangelist was coincidentally holding a meeting in our neighbourhood to which we took Fabian. He nonchalantly sauntered up to receive prayer and returned declaring himself healed and saying ' we can go home now'. This is the simple faith of a child that Jesus spoke of – unlike his anxious parents wondering will He heal or won't He? We hope to make time for special trips over the course of the summer, for instance we all enjoyed a day at Alton Towers courtesy of Rays of Sunshine. I'm proud to say the girls and I rode the infamous 'Smiler' and memories of our trip to Disneyland came flooding back – literally – when all got soaked on the flume ride. Fabian's new raised garden has exploded with life with the sunshine and rain and he loves tending it. It's a well-known cliche', but each day is a gift.

AUGUST 8, 2014

Change of course

Since I began this blog three years ago, I have always held to the notion that a half full attitude is better than a half empty one. Not just an empty sentiment – the book of Proverbs warns us that 'that which I fear shall come upon me'. I knew too, though, that there would likely be entries when it would be hard to be positive and this is certainly one of those.

It had been looking uncertain last time as everyone suspected the treatment was failing because the disease level had increased, though we were hoping some of the T cells still remained. Sadly, though, it was confirmed by the latest bone marrow check that there has been a further rise in blast cells (visible now at cellular level) and that no T cells are detectable. Naturally, we and the medical team are perplexed and hugely disappointed, especially given Fabian's positive – albeit transient-response to the previous batch of T cells. No one can say for sure why this time round has failed. It may be that his own immune cells have since developed antibodies that destroyed the modified cells, or possibly that the leukemia has evolved into a different variant that isn't identifiable by the T cell receptors. This news now requires a change of course since there is no alternative treatment available that has curative intent, so we are left with disease control and symptom care as our only option. Nowadays, this can be extremely effective in suppressing many cancers, although we never wanted to settle for disease management and have always fought to obtain whatever would offer Fabian the best hope of a cure. In this respect, we were encouraged by our consultant who said we have been the best advocates for Fabian we could be (or isn't that just being a parent?). In the meantime, who knows what breakthroughs are just around the corner? Already, the use of genome sequencing is leading to so-called personalised drugs that will one day render chemotherapy obsolete. Immunotherapy too, is improving as more evidence, particularly from the U.S. studies, comes through. I guess, though, if Fabian was writing this he would be shouting 'no more drugs and hospital stays!' and that is something we must respect. You reach a place where the equation says 'quality of life>quantity of treatment'. We are now into the vacation period (or staycation in our case) but Fabian's has already been interrupted by 5 days in our local hospital because of (another) infection. At least the ensuite facility and room service was excellent. During this time, he had to attend a daycare appointment at Great Ormond Street so they sent him by ambulance with full blues and twos. The usual 90 minute journey took just 30! However, we hope to fit in more exciting day trips if this period of glorious weather persists. My closing thought is to remember the occasion recorded in Luke 8 of Jesus healing Jairus' daughter, a child the same age as Fabian. When He was delayed and the girl died, they said to Him 'why bother the teacher anymore?". But He merely told them not to fear and went on to raise her to life. I like that. Jesus always has the last word regardless of our human understanding. And He never minds being bothered. Have great holidays!

This sucks!

Time for a polite rant – this disease sucks. Whatever we have thrown at it, the thing reinvents itself and comes back stronger. Medically, they call it clonal evolution so whereas in the early days the leukaemia had 'one cancerous head' there are now many, a bit like the Hydra of Greek myth. I was reading Fabian's most recent haematology report and it runs to 15 pages of lab analysis! And this is a fraction of what a complete genome sequence would generate. We are indeed 'fearfully and wonderfully made'.

Well, the latest news is that Fabian came down last week with a serious infection that turned out to be an eColi. His blood counts are shot to pieces just now because of disease and chemo, hence his susceptibility to this commonly found bacterium. It has taken a while to stabilise him with antibiotics but he's slowly winning the fight and the doctors acknowledge he is one tough cookie. Of course, being an in-patient is so miserable for him and he has been rather down at times. My usual attempts to elicit a smile (like wearing a bedpan on my head) have lost their lustre but if his temperature holds steady we may get a few hours home leave this weekend. So having now reached the limit of what conventional treatment can do, we have been looking into taking an integrative approach and possibly combining or replacing chemo with alternative therapies. There is no shortage of material on the Net in this regard, much of which has to be run through the 'quackwatch' filter. That said, God has clearly put healing properties in many herbs and plants and these have been around long before allopathic medicine and the pharmaceuticals. Interestingly, one evidence-based agent is the highly toxic oleander plant, known as Anvirzel in drug form. We also like it because it bears the same name as our eldest! Equally, there are more biological therapies coming onstream which are antibody targeted treatments but probably no more effective than 'good' old chemo. We certainly would not put Fabian through any more hospitalisation without far greater certainty of a good outcome.

During the sunny days we managed to fit in some enjoyable events including CarFest, Lego Show, BBC Good Food Show and a helicopter flight. Fabian's vegetable garden abounds and he has produced what must be the largest courgette I have ever seen. The chickens and rabbits bore offspring and our apple tree has gone bananas (with apples).

I am not going to say anything other than that we are in a difficult place, but never alone. His rod and staff, they comfort us (Ps 23) and His promises are yes and amen.

SEPTEMBER 21, 2014

Infections, decisions and our big G

Torrid times for Fabian as he succumbs to more infections resulting in three hospital admissions in the past two weeks. This is a predictable outcome of him having close to zero white cells and completely zero neutrophils. Without this natural protection every bug or virus is a potential killer. These usually present with an all too familiar spike in temperature and we have to grab the overnight bag and head to our local (hospital, not bar). We had a serious scare when during one night Fabian's heart rate dropped below 40 and his BP shot up. Thankfully, it stabilised over time but doctors were left scratching their heads as to what the cause was despite a raft of diagnostics such as ECG, X ray and CT scan. Most infections are linked to his intravenous lines and PEG (gastric tube). These are particularly hard to shift and being in constant use for meds mean one simply exacerbates the problem. The local hospital is generally very good but they don't deal with enough oncology related illnesses to anticipate the sort of complications Fabian presents. Our own knowledge of what to do is often key to making the right intervention but we were completely caught out recently whilst enjoying a restaurant meal. Fabian had been to wash hands and returned with a large damp patch on his shirt. We assumed he had splashed himself but subsequently discovered that the PEG had loosened and his stomach was leaking. Having to patch him up urgently in front of the other diners no doubt spoilt their appetites!

In terms of treatment, we've agreed by necessity to stop oral chemo and tick over on vincristine and steroids until his counts recover. That will reduce risk of infection but won't necessarily stem the spread of disease. It's a case of the lesser of two evils but if his marrow can recover, we can start to use immune boosting supplements that are anti-cancer agents too. We are also in the 'valley of decision' about whether to apply for further experimental therapy. I'm referring here to blinatumamab, a monoclonal antibody that is achieving remission within two weeks for at least one third of ALL patients who are using this drug. The flip side to this is potentially life-threatening side effects that kick in if the drug is working! The key attraction, though, is that it's a new and different weapon to wield against Fabian's subversive leukaemia and therefore stands a better chance of succeeding than simply repeating chemo. We need to be sure, though, that this is in the family's best interest. All of us are affected by the ongoing disruption and emotional rollercoaster but then any parent reading this knows we are hard-wired never to give up the fight for a child and I'm reminded of a certain president who famously said; 'if we do nothing, we run the risk of failure'.

Fabian remains sanguine throughout these ordeals and his good humour and charming wit make him a firm favourite with the medical staff. We continue to fit in the odd day trip or special event, most recently the concourse de elegance collection of famous cars at Hampton Court and a corporate activity centre where we all donned cams and took part in a 'battlefield live' laser fight. September is UK childhood cancer awareness month and the many stories publicised highlight just how many ordinary families like ours are fighting the big C. Before this all happened, I would never have paused to think about it, but now we're on the inside looking out it's been a revelation.

Please keep sending your prayers for Fabian upward; there's a big G fighting for him.

OCTOBER 15, 2014

The longest night

I've learnt not to assume when I wake up that I have any idea or control over what unexpected event might happen that day. In other words, to take nothing for granted. Because when I went to work as normal last week, I had no idea that by the end of the day I would be holding my son as doctors fought to save his life. So what happened? Fabian had returned home a few days before following another spell in hospital that resulted in having to remove his Hickman line which had become infected. For the first time in years he now required cannulas and blood tests using needles; not pleasant when he had been used to plug'n play intravenous lines. He seemed well enough that morning but later spiked a temperature and was duly readmitted for another cycle of antibiotics. Nothing unusual in that, except as they infused the first dose,

Fabian went into septic shock and this sent his vital signs into orbit. In just a few minutes, his heart rate hit 240, temperature reached 40.1 and there was no discernible blood pressure. Coupled with this came a powerful attack of rigors – convulsive shaking as the body attempts to raise its temperature. Doctors injected him with a series of water boluses in an attempt to resuscitate his BP but with limited success. He was put into the dependency unit, a sort of ICU-lite and hooked up to oxygen and a cluster of monitoring lines. As the night wore on, his BP dropped further and on repeated occasions, doctors took us aside to decide whether they should transfer Fabian across to St George's ICU. It was clear they felt they had reached their own limits and that he would otherwise succumb within a few hours if not moved. The ICU option itself was high risk as he might not have tolerated the powerful drugs they use, not to mention the journey across London. Well, we agonised over this but ultimately decided he should remain put, believing that the many prayers being said around the world would carry him through. One deep concern was that our eldest daughter, Oli, was 300 miles away at University, so we had to make a difficult call and ask her to catch the first available train back which she willingly did, much to Fabian's delight. The rest of that night seemed interminable. We dozed next to him, keeping a half-closed eye on the monitors for signs of his BP stabilising. I can't recall the exact time when I heard the nurse say; 'It's risen slightly', but from that moment we knew he had turned the corner and with that came a huge sense of peace. Fast forward to morning, and Fabian was sitting up asking for breakfast! The doctors and nurses all took turns to pop in and were genuinely shocked but delighted at his rapid recovery. Oli by then had turned up and might have wondered what the urgency had been about. However, a further setback later that day was that his gastrostomy wound opened up and rather dramatically, poured forth a large amount of bile and blood. The sight of it was very distressing and Fabian was in agony. Although properly dressed now, it remains a real concern and he's unable to eat or drink normally until the wound closes up. The original infection is a lot more stubborn and of course, underlying the immediate issues is the disease itself which continues to wipe out any healthy white cells he has. Our plans for blinatumamab (excellent word for scrabble) are therefore on hold, perhaps for good? We had previously made the day trip to Sheffield to discuss this drug option with the team there and felt on balance, it offered a worthwhile attempt at getting back into remission. The odds are low, but better than none.

A few days before this incident we heard sadly that yet another Marsden boy known to us had lost his fight. By God's mercy, we still have our Fabian because He numbers our days, not because his days are numbered.

OCTOBER 31, 2014

Pain and awe

Having pulled through life-threatening septicaemia, Fabian has had to endure a number of further complications in rapid succession. The worst of these has been his stoma which has caused no end of problems. Ironically, we agreed to have this inserted last year to provide a safer and more convenient method for his feeds and meds. Latterly though, the site became infected and opened up as a gaping wound, with stomach contents leaking out. The actual catheter ended up inside his stomach (a first for the doctors) and after an anxious few days we were relieved when it came out the other end fully intact! Apparently, this incident is being written up in a medical journal. The 'gunshot wound', as Fabian calls it, needs a daily change of dressing but is stubbornly refusing to heal on account of his low white count. We can't consider further treatment whilst this is the case so it's a nasty case of chicken and egg.

Thankfully, he is now an outpatient although hospital trips for reviews and blood products are routine. The high disease level is causing Fabian more or less continuous pain. This manifests as an aching deep in his bones and by all accounts is worse than muscular pain which could otherwise be simply relieved by heat patches. Instead, we are having to give morphine via slow or quick release methods. Witnessing your child in pain is frankly gut-wrenching. But the downside to morphine is the fatigue and nausea side effects which tend to knock him out for long periods. Still, our incredible son keeps picking himself up and showing the resilience of which we are so in awe. We've begun a regimen of supplements to help restore his metabolism and lack of a normal diet. It's a shame the healthiest ones taste the worst but he has become resigned to taking them without too much coercion. The years of toxic treatment have debilitated his frail body and I can only wonder how we will ever rebuild him, but I will leave no stone unturned in researching the best natural products to help do this.

Despite the gloomy tone of this entry, I want to commend the tremendous answers to worldwide prayers that have lifted our spirits as we have seen Fabian exceed medical expectation. The bible tells us that faith the size of a mustard seed can move mountains, so God is not trying to make it difficult for us to believe! More anon.

NOVEMBER 17, 2014

Remembrance Day – our fighter goes home

I forgot to wear a poppy this year nor did I observe the
minute silence at 11. I was too engrossed holding
Fabian's hand and gazing into his beautiful face as he
lay peacefully dying in a hospital bed, his respiratory
rate becoming slower by the hour.

Just 4 days before, he had been at home, weak but
stable, enjoying visitors to the house. That week had
begun with an unplanned trip to Legoland. It was the
final day of their season and thankfully, one last chance
for him to enjoy his favourite theme park. The next few
days were spent in daycare having the usual reviews and
blood products. Fabian agreed to having an NG tube
fitted so that we could run overnight feeds. He had
effectively stopped eating since the last sepsis in early
October and as the gastrostomy had failed too, was
slowly starving himself. This was a daily source of
anguish for us, so having the tube back was a relief,
short-lived as things turned out. Then we were
telephoned on Friday to be told that a blood culture
showed another gram-negative infection was present.
We immediately started oral antibiotics but within a few
hours he had deteriorated to such an extent that we
needed an ambulance ride to A&E where a team of
nurses and doctors worked feverishly to stabilise the
developing sepsis. Déjà vue, I thought, as Fabian lay
there on oxygen support, heart racing, BP falling. At
such times, the doctors take you aside to discuss
'options'. The gravity of this situation was made clear.
But being the fighter that he was, Fabian made it out of
emergency and onto the ward and the immediate threat
to life was over. However, this time his BP did not fully
recover and this set in motion the consequential failure
of his organs as they were gradually starved of oxygen.

111

Alongside this, Fabian's disease symptoms were rising fast, so inevitably he required a morphine pump to manage this. His agonising bony pain was thankfully subdued by this potent drug and he slipped into a semi-comatose state.

We had started to call friends and family to visit and many came. Fabian knew this and attempted to rally, giving us flickers of hope that the infection might yet be fought off. In truth, his kidneys had failed and fluid and toxins were steadily building inside, placing pressure on his heart and lungs. They attempted inserting a urine catheter, a most undignified procedure, but strangely only after they withdrew it did Fabian wee! He just continued to surprise. Then came a seizure. This was both unexpected and frightening, yet once again he pulled through with no immediate signs of neurological damage and continued communicating with small sounds and hand movements.

I guess any denial that we were at the so-called end of life stage finally left us once they stopped further transfusions. These were simply adding to the fluid build-up and exacerbating that problem. I requested they keep up the antibiotics which they did more out of compassion than for any meaningful purpose. In any event, his PIC line then failed so we lost all intravenous access.

Now Fabian had been asking to go home and it became our focus to make this dying wish a reality. We also had the option of transferring to a nearby children's hospice where practical support would be on hand. Time wasn't on our side, though, and we were advised the very act of transferring him could be fatal. So we agreed to stay the Monday night and reassess things in the morning. That night was agonising. Our girls were with us as we cuddled round Fabian's bedside, speaking loving words to him as he lay serenely, eyes closed, his breathing by now, alarmingly slow. Fluid in his lungs was making this quite laboured but he maintained this minute by minute. I glanced at my watch, noting it was past midnight and was now Remembrance Day. Would this be the day we would never forget? Somehow, we still kept praying for healing. Faith in extreme adversity is a powerful force and we knew God raised even from death as He did so through Jesus on earth. Well, we. didn't witness a miracle that night, but by morning there was a noticeable improvement in Fabian's breathing, enough for the decision to agree to discharge him and go home. There is considerable bureaucracy in such a situation and this delayed matters by vital hours, but by early afternoon Fabian was safely back where he had wanted. It was so very timely. His best friend had just arrived and was able to make one last piece of Lego and place this in his hand. Just a few short hours later Fabian drew his last, surrounded by our presence and love as we said goodbye to him on this earth.

He now lays at rest, surrounded by treasured items as we await his service of remembrance. It will be a fitting occasion to mark the passing of a unique little boy whose short life touched and impacted so many, from royalty downwards. A huge sinkhole, as it were, has opened in our family but we have the assured, bible-backed guarantee of meeting him again and in this, we take comfort for now.

So to the many thousands of followers of my family's journey recorded through this blog, you have been a silent, continuous support to us, especially to Fabian knowing as he did that he was known and loved worldwide. I dedicate this site and it's future development to his memory and pray that our story will be a resource to comfort, support and encourage any who must tragically face the terminal illness of a child. Please post a comment below that we can record these in a book of condolence.

"Friends, we want you to know the truth about those who have died, so that you will not be sad, as are those who have no hope." 1 Thess 4:13

He will be missed, but always remembered.
Fabian Luke Sebastian Bate 02/03/02 to 11/11/14

-----------------------oOo-----------------------

MARCH 14TH, 2015

Raining in my heart
"There's a grief that can't be spoken, there's a pain that goes on and on". The words from the melancholic song in Les Miserables are never more true for us than now. Its's been a little over 4 months. On March 2nd we commemorated what would have been Fabian's 13th birthday. Having already been blessed with three teenagers I wish with all my heart for Fabian to have been my fourth. His loss is truly devastating and profoundly sad for all those that knew him. I'm told that the basic instinct to live and get on helps get you through but then not to block the pain through overdoing it. Here at home, we are surrounded by physical reminders of his presence; toys, clothes, places he played. The many photos and videos we have of him are bitter sweet, evoking an aching sadness together with sweet memories. We've left his room much as he last left it, Lego kits, hot wheels and an array of his baseball caps all still in their place. It is a sanctuary where I feel close to Fabian, both there and at his raised vegetable garden that brought so him much delight in his final months. The huge marrow that was his pride

and joy amazingly still lies there, recognisable but gradually rotting. When it finally decomposes, another tangible connection with Fabian will have gone and only the precious photo we have of him holding it will remain.

So having commenced this lifelong journey of grief, what have I learnt so far? As a Christian who believes God can and does heal, how has my faith been affected? I'm quick to recognise that this life experience is hardly unique and many, many others have travelled the same road and written more eloquently than I ever could about child bereavement. A good example being the best seller 'When bad things happen to good people' (note the title states "when" not 'if') which certainly challenges the usual Christian response to suffering. The fact is, for more than 8 years many prayers for Fabians' healing were said in good faith. And yet he did not live. We certainly accept Gods sovereign will, but one could be forgiven for asking how the death of a child could be Gods' will. That will be my first question when we meet. Yet we were right to continually pray for a cure but could never assume God would reverse the spread of disease for our son when He does not intervene miraculously for many other 'good' and 'righteous' people fighting terminal cancer.

Despite the outcome, we felt Him with us every step of the way and this was evident through the love and support of those around us, for as someone has said, human beings are God's language. So, the skilful doctor, dedicated nurse, comforting pastor, devoted friend and supportive family member were all daily answers to those prayers during Fabian's journey. And you know our palliative care nurse shared what I felt was a profound truth just hours after Fabian passed as we sat together going through practicalities. She observed that in her work with the dying she sees many small miracles, but few big ones. I think this is what we sometimes undervalue, the small victories and breakthroughs of which there were many in Fabian's life despite him not getting 'the big one'. Don't get me wrong, I would selfishly exchange all of this just to have our son back, but as time passes maybe a bigger picture will emerge. For instance, I am starting to see that all of Fabian's unlived years have transferred to us, his family, especially his three siblings who have their whole lives ahead with which to live out a legacy for their brother. Indeed, the three areas in which each of them individually excels – science, music and art, will I feel sure, be that little bit richer for the greater strength of character and purpose that the children now have. We see signs of this already; Oleander recently chose to research a technical aspect of leukaemia diagnosis for her dissertation. Ben has been inspired to compose music in his brother's memory; Cassia draws and paints exquisitely from the heart.

To other news, the long-awaited film featuring Fabian and two other children who underwent treatment at Great Ormond Street Hospital will be shown on ITV1 sometime in April. They've called it 'Raining in my heart' (though we're not sure why!). Follow the Twitter feed at #raininginmyheart for further announcements. We've seen the final edit and feel truly blessed to have such a beautiful record in film of his last year with us (have the tissues to hand, though). We're also moving forward with the Memorial Fund which will shortly receive charitable status. You can now donate via PayPal from the Lego link on this site.

Let's continue to remember Fabian - forever in our hearts.

Eleven Eleven

Returning to my blog on 11/11 four years on brings mixed emotions. I recall so well the pain and sadness of charting our journey with Fabian in those last two years of his life, juxtaposed with times of relief and fun together. So now, on this anniversary of his passing, I'm ready to return and update faithful followers with our news since.

There are many analogies used to describe grief and they all have their place. Here's one; grief is like a watch – something you wear unconsciously but occasionally check – it's there all the time. We've certainly handled grief differently within the family. There are no rights or wrongs, no better or worse. The children adapted quickly, trying to forget and move on in their lives as they pursue their individual career paths. But they hold an unstated anger within that life is unfair. I can't disagree. But as parents, the process is different for us. It's hard to move on lest we feel his memory is forgotten. We've kept his room much as it was together with all his possessions. It is a sanctuary to sit there from time to time and let those items trigger sweet memories of happy times together. Over the years, we've attended several bereavement groups and courses and often come away feeling surprised at how well we seem to be coping when compared to others. But then, of course, we have a hope that we will be reunited together in heaven. What a hope! Lydia tends Fabian's grave with unstinting devotion. Dare I say it, there seems to be a competitive edge amongst the children's graves as to whose is the most immaculate. We deliberated an excessively long time over the nature of his headstone and inscription thereon. It had to be fitting and lasting. Unlike an elderly relative, a young child's grave is likely to be visited over a far greater period, as siblings will have many more years ahead of them to do this. Fortunately, one of the many treats Fabian had been given was the opportunity to have a life-cast made at Elstree Studios and having this mould gave us the option to commission a bust of his head. We were anxious it needed to be sculpted sensitively and present a good resemblance as there would be no second chance if we weren't happy with the result. Well, any fears were simply blown away when it was unveiled to us. The cast, in white marble, beautifully captures Fabian's wistful smile and he looks peaceful. It sits atop a rather dominant granite stone and will no doubt weather a century of outdoor exposure. To commemorate its' installation, we held an unveiling service at the grave to which many came and shared this time. Two friends, both professional violinists, played and Fabian's old headteacher gave a short message. The sun shone beautifully as it did that day we buried him.

One obvious positive since 2014 has been the founding of a charity in Fabian's memory. Fabian's Childhood Cancer Trust (www.fabianstrust.org.uk) is ably run by Lydia with help from volunteers who support her in a range of fund-raising events. The charity has been nominated charity of the year by several retailers and uses its funds to provide treat bags and breaks for parents of children with life-limiting conditions. Funds are also used to support research into leukaemia treatment being undertaken at the Irving Laboratory for Cancer research in Newcastle. Fund-raising is both demanding and time-consuming and we are always touched by the generosity of those who volunteer to support this work.

We've always monitored the progress of the ground-breaking CAR-T immunotherapy trial that Fabian pioneered, It has been heartening to read this treatment was subsequently approved by the FDA in the U.S. and just recently, becoming a first-line treatment for childhood leukaemia here in the UK. Indeed, we found ourselves unwitting guests on the Victoria Derbyshire BBC1 programme to talk about our feelings when this was announced. Bitter sweet, of course, as we wonder whether the newer version might have cured him as it is now doing for a much higher proportion of children. The interview was conducted by Skype and we supposed it was on radio rather than TV so it was a shock to see ourselves on the screen watching later on catch-up!

So today, the nation remembers that momentous day 100 years ago, of the Armistice and it is fitting that this year it should fall on the Sunday so that many can attend church services across the land. We will, of course, be wearing our green poppies, remembering both those who gave their lives and Fabian whose life was taken.

.

Acknowledgements

The retelling of our story through the blog is accurate based on my memories of the events, though some inaccuracies or perceptions may have slipped through.

We would like to acknowledge and thank the three consultant physicians who between them managed Fabian's care during his 8 and half years of treatment; Dr Donna Lancaster, Paediatric Oncologist at the Royal Marsden, Surrey, Dr Persis Amrolia, Professor of Transplantation Immunology at Great Ormond Street Hospital and Dr Andrew Winrow, Consultant Paediatrician at Kingston Hospital. To the many nurses (too many to name!) we also extend heartfelt thanks for the love and care shown to use as a family. Special mention must go to Bianca Effemey, CEO of Momentum Children's Charity. Momentum provided extra special support not only in person by Bianca but in the many treats and trips afforded to us – a truly inspirational charity. And lest we forget, CLIC Sargent, based at the Royal Marsden who offered us counselling, bereavement support and the wonderful 'red letter' away days for bereaved Mums and Dads.

Our journey was shared with wider family, friends, school and work colleagues. Staff and pupils at Fabian's school, Cornerstone were especially dear to us, always remembering Fabian in prayer and creating a wonderful 'remembrance room' at the school after his passing.

Finally, to our older children, Oleander, Ben and Cassia-Rose who were robbed for a large part of their childhood by having to live with cancer in the family. Their grief at losing a brother is unfathomable and is our deepest regret as their parents.

This was just something we couldn't fix.

About the authors

Darrell is married to Lydia and they live in the town of East Molesey, Surrey with their French bulldog, Rocco. They attend St Marys Church, East Molesey. They have three adult children, Oleander, Ben and Cassia-Rose.

Lydia and her father are co-founders of Fabian's Childhood Cancer Trust, a charity dedicated to supporting families with a child diagnosed with cancer. The charity provides family breaks and 'Treat bags' for parents staying on the wards of the Children's cancer unit at the Royal Marsden Hospital. These contain essentials for a hospital stay plus some special treats to let them know that someone cares. Funds are also used to support research in childhood acute lymphoblastic leukaemia.

Fabian was one of the very first children in the UK to receive the CAR-T immunotherapy trial run by Prof Persis Amrolia at Great Ormond Street Hospital. The trial attracted media interest and Fabian was filmed over the course of a year during this treatment and featured along with two other children in the ITV documentary 'Raining in my Heart'. The producers kindly made a short film in memory of Fabian that was shown at his funeral and can be viewed at https://youtu.be/3oC_KdZ9o-8

Fabian had attracted earlier media interest when in 2011 he met the Duke and Duchess of Cambridge during their opening of the new children's' unit at the Royal Marsden Hospital, Surrey. Kate and William subsequently wrote to Fabian on several occasions and this generated much press interest and some TV appearances.

Contact the authors at darrellbate@gmail.com

Printed in Great Britain
by Amazon